THE HIGH PRIESTS OF WAR

Leroy G. Hoberly

ABOUT THE COVER . . .

At the top left is an image of a statue of the Virgin Mary which an Israeli army tank fired upon on March 14, 2002, shattering the nose and slicing off the hands. The hated statue stood high above the Roman Catholic Holy Family Hospital and Orphanage in Jerusalem adjacent to a Vatican flag. The Israelis fired on the statue at close range. It was not an accident. It was an act of hatred.

And hatred likewise is expressed in the violent image of the hanging of Haman, taken from a Jewish religious artifact. One of the first of many enemies of the Jewish people, Haman's assassination by execution is celebrated on the holiday of Purim, which—just coincidentally, it is said—marked the onslaught of the war against Iraq, a point noted in Jewish newspapers that referred to Saddam Hussein as a modern-day Haman.

At middle-level left is a relief from Rome's Arch of Titus, recalling the sacking of Jerusalem by the Romans and the triumphant seizure of the Jewish temple's menorah.

The fall of Jerusalem—one of the great disasters of Jewish history—was another of the endless series of events marking the conflict of the Middle East that is still being fought out today.

At mid-level right is Ariel Sharon, the brutal Israeli caesar whose hard-line policies against the Christian and Muslim Palestinian Arabs are highly popular among his fellow countrymen and much admired by most American Jewish leaders and their allies in the neo-conservative movement, despite significant grass-roots Jewish opposition notwithstanding.

Sharon's goal of achieving "Greater Israel" is part and parcel of the neo-conservative agenda and the ultimate in hate and imperialism.

At the bottom, from left to right, are Paul Wolfowitz, Richard Perle, William Kristol and Henry Kissinger, perhaps the most powerful figures in the neo-conservative network that orchestrated the tragic U.S. war against Iraq. The neo-conservative High Priests of War dream of establishing a world empire and intend to use America's young people as the cannon fodder to accomplish their goal.

That *is* hate—and we *must* fight hate.

THE HIGH PRIESTS OF WAR

The Secret History of How America's "Neo-Conservative" Trotskyites Came to Power and Orchestrated the War Against Iraq as the First Step in Their Drive for Global Empire

BY MICHAEL COLLINS PIPER

AMERICAN FREE PRESS
Washington, D.C.
www.americanfreepress.net

The High Priests of War

First Printing: February 2004
Second Printing: May 2004
Third Printing: August 2004
Fourth Printing: October 2004

Published by: American Free Press
645 Pennsylvania Avenue, SE, Suite 100
Washington, D.C. 20003
1-888-699-6397
www.americanfreepress.net

Library of Congress Control Number: 2004092376
ISBN Number: 0-9745484-1-3
© 2004 by Michael Collins Piper

To contact the author:
Michael Collins Piper
P.O. Box 15728
Washington, DC 20003
Email: piperm@lycos.com
Tel: (202) 544-5977

Special thanks to John Tiffany for an excellent copy editing job, as always. Looking for the best copy editor in the world? It's John. He'll drive you crazy with his questions and his nit-picking, but he gets the job done. (John can be contacted at xuou@yahoo.com) Any errors in this book are mine alone. It simply means I ignored John's sage advice.

Also thanks to Lamis Andoni for permission to quote from her excellent exposition regarding the nefarious record of Bernard Lewis.

Special acknowledgment is due Bill and Kathleen Christison and Anis Shivani whose hard-hitting commentary on counterpunch.org added a great deal to my efforts.

The work of John Sugg at atlanta.creativeloafing.com is a "must" for anyone interested in the intrigues of the powers-that-be.

And the importance of the work of Andrew Bacevich, particularly his book, *American Empire*, cannot be overstated.

Thanks to those and many others who have dared to tackle the most masterful intriguers ever to assume such immense power in America.

—MCP

"BAD PLACES" . . .

"The list of possible Bad Places does not begin with haunted houses and end with haunted hotels; there have been horror stories written about haunted railroad stations, automobiles, meadows, office buildings. The list is endless, and probably all of it goes back to the caveman who had to move out of his hole in the rock because he heard what sounded like voices back there in the shadows. Whether they were actual voices or the voices of the wind is a question we still ask ourselves on dark nights."

—HORROR MASTER STEPHEN KING

The High Priests of War is a non-fiction book that resembles a Gothic horror novel, a classic tale of a haunted house and the evil spirits that dwell within, the story of a wealthy young king—scion of a famous family—ensconced in a stately palace and endowed with great powers, yet surrounded, even possessed, by malevolent demonic forces manipulating him from "back there in the shadows."

But the high priests of war exist in real life. The damage these neo-conservative war-mongers are doing to America and the world is immense.

If these neo-conservatives continue in their reign of ruin, we should not be surprised to see the White House end up looking once again as it did after being gutted by British torches in 1814: whether the consequence of a popular rebellion by angry patriotic Americans or the result of an attack by foreign forces determined to stop dead the intrigues of the high priests of war.

One thing is certain: ***The time has come. Something has to be done . . .***

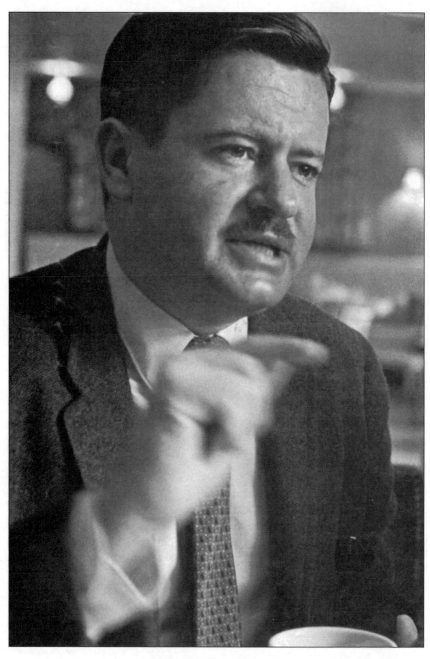

ANDREW ST. GEORGE
OCTOBER 25, 1923 – MAY 2, 2001

DEDICATION

To the one and only
ANDREW ST. GEORGE

—The fearless journalist who pioneered coverage of the strange intrigues of the neo-conservative warmongers long before they came to be acknowledged by the major media as front-line players on the global stage.

A valued friend and a memorable figure, a raconteur like no other, a bon vivant and a loving husband and proud father, Andrew was a mentor with a track record as an international correspondent few could match.

Andrew's first-on-the-scene reportage exposed the neo-conservatives as the genuine menace to world peace that they are.

—MICHAEL COLLINS PIPER

A United States Senator Speaks Out:
Why Americans are <u>really</u> dying in Iraq . . .

"With 760 dead in Iraq and over 3,000 maimed for life, home folks continue to argue why we are in Iraq—and how to get out . . . Even President Bush acknowledges that Saddam Hussein had nothing to do with 9-11. . . Of course there were no weapons of mass destruction. Israel's intelligence, Mossad, knows what's going on in Iraq. They are the best. They have to know. Israel's survival depends on knowing. Israel long since would have taken us to the weapons of mass destruction if there were any or if they had been removed. With Iraq no threat, why invade a sovereign country? The answer: President Bush's policy to secure Israel."

> —U.S. Senator Ernest F. Hollings (D-S.C.)
> Writing in *The Charleston Post and Courier*, May 6, 2004

(For making these forthright remarks, in a column in which he also specifically named several of the "high priests of war" described in this book, Sen. Hollings—a longtime friend of the U.S. military—was harshly denounced by the Anti-Defamation League and a host of politicians eager to curry favor with the Israeli lobby. Yet, just shortly before, a respected Jewish newspaper, *Forward*, stated that Israel had benefited from the Iraq war—"uniquely" it said—and that Israeli intelligence had provided information used by the Bush administration to justify the invasion of Iraq. See below for what *Forward* said.)

Leading Jewish Newspaper Explains:
Israel "uniquely benefited" from Iraq war . . .

"On the eve of the war, Israel was a quiet but enthusiastic supporter of America's war plans. Saddam Hussein's military power, it was universally agreed, made him one of the Jewish state's most dangerous adversaries . . . His overthrow was seen as eliminating Israel's most serious existential threat . . . [and Israel] eagerly cooperated . . . sharing information on Iraqi capabilities and intentions . . . meant to help the American action . . . . But because Israel uniquely benefited from a war that is increasingly controversial in America and around the world, fears of speaking out have grown even stronger than they were before the war."

> —The New York-based Jewish weekly *Forward*, April 16, 2004

FOREWORD: Authority Without Responsibility . . .

Although much has recently been written about the intrigues of the neo-conservatives who rule the roost in the administration of George W. Bush, *The High Priests of War* is by far the most comprehensive work on the subject available today, particularly in that it explores the neo-conservative agenda from a highly important historic perspective that has generally been ignored in the heat of current debate.

It can accurately be said that the author, Michael Collins Piper, was one of the first journalists on the face of the planet to have recognized the neo-conservative infiltration of the upper ranks of the American political and intelligence mechanisms and then—as far back as the early 1980s—began writing about the phenomenon.

Piper duly credits our mutual longtime friend and colleague, the late Andrew St. George—to whom this book is dedicated—with having pioneered the first significant news reportage on the neo-conservatives, and it can rightly be said that St. George is the literary "godfather" of this important book.

Tackling the most important political problem of our age and skillfully analyzing its origins, naming names and describing the agenda and the misdeeds of the highly astute and closely inter-connected group which is dexterously pulling the strings that manipulate the marionettes on the political stage, *The High Priests of War* is a landmark work.

The neoconservatives have accomplished the supreme political feat: they have the authority but not the responsibility for the disastrous course of American history, immune to their misdeeds and the responsibility therefor, thanks to their controlled press.

Thus, as our country reels from disaster to disaster, the public is either told by the press how wonderful it all is or replaceable politicians are blamed for it while the neocons only tighten their hold.

This sordid scenario is unknown to all but a tiny handful of American patriots. If a significant number of Americans can be awakened to the political reality described by Michael Collins Piper so clearly in this book, the exposure alone will put an end to the conspiracy.

—W. A. CARTO

"It's time to declare war on The High Priests of War"

Although most—but certainly not all—American anti-communists were sincere, it is vital to now face the sad and uncomfortable truth: the Cold War was largely a fraud.

While the average American was being told to fear the Soviet Union, America's biggest bankers and industrialists were engaged in extensive trade and other lucrative deals with the Communist Party bosses. And the U.S. government itself was making vast amounts of defense technology and other data available to our purported rival. So yes, the Cold War was very much a fraud.

To finally understand and accept that difficult reality makes it possible for us to reassess the globalist madness of the last 50 years and to prepare for the real battle for survival that lies ahead.

Until Americans are finally prepared to acknowledge that the anti-communist frenzy to which so many devoted their energies was effectively so misdirected and fruitless, there is no sense in fighting any further. For generations we were fighting perceived "enemies" abroad, but the real enemy was here at home—infiltrating and seizing power in the upper ranks of the American national security and intelligence apparatus.

As evidence put forth in this book makes clear, the Soviet threat—however great it may have been at one point in time—was, in more recent decades, clearly on the downward spiral, its strength diminishing. However, the neo-conservative forces, eager to exploit fears of Soviet power in order to play out their own parochial agenda, were exaggerating both Soviet military might and Soviet intentions. And it must be said, quite correctly, that the foundation of the neo-conservative agenda—from the beginning—was not just the security, but also the imperial advancement, of the state of Israel.

We must abandon the archaic rhetoric of the past and focus on the real threat to America—and to the sovereignty of all nations and peoples: the power-mad imperial forces that are bent on using American resources and military might to enforce a global police state under the control of a select few: the international elite and their bought-and-paid-for politicians, unprincipled bureaucrats, and the media shills who glorify and attempt to popularize the agenda of the would-be rulers of a Global Plantation that its proponents have stylized as the New World Order.

Although *The Spotlight* was quite on the mark when it dared to suggest, upon the fall of the Soviet empire, that "communism is dead," there were those relentless hold-outs who refused to face it. "Oh no," cried the John Birchers, "communism isn't really dead. It's just a ruse. The reds are going underground, just waiting for the opportunity to strike."

The Birchers and their like-minded throwbacks still believe that Josef Stalin is hiding in a Kremlin closet, ready to jump out and say "boo." Yet, ironically, only now are the Birchers coming to recognize that the neo-conservatives—whom they promoted for years in the pages of their journals such as *Review of the News* and *The New American*—are hardly conventional "conservative patriots" in any sense of the term.

The same crowd that rattled its sabers against "the communist threat" has now begun to substitute "the Islamic threat" as the new danger to be vanquished. This comes as no surprise. For years, during the Cold War, American "conservatives" (especially the Birchers) freely (and falsely) declared repeatedly that the Palestine Liberation Organization was part of a "Soviet-backed terror network," the facts notwithstanding.

And if truth be told, it is no accident that these myths about the PLO received their widest propagation in the writings of a pro-Israel neo-conservative ideologue, Claire Sterling, whose now-infamous "study," *The Terror Network*, became the virtual bible of the Israeli lobby in its campaign to discredit the Palestinian nationalist cause.

Now, in the name of "fighting terrorism," the conservative anti-communist stalwarts have lent their support to the establishment of a police state here at home as a way of "safeguarding liberty."

In this regard, note that more than 50 years ago—in the early days of the Cold War—that ex-CIA man William F. Buckley, Jr., the soon-to-be self-appointed "leader" of the American "conservative" movement, laid it on the line. Writing in *Commonweal* on January 25, 1952 Buckley said that he was willing to support "Big Government" for "the duration [of the Cold War] because—he proclaimed—only "a totalitarian bureaucracy within our shores" could assure total victory over the communist menace.

The anti-communist Cold War is now over, but the anti-Islamic (so-called "anti-terrorist") Hot War is now under way. And here on American shores we have a new Department of Homeland Security aiming to run roughshod on American liberties all in the guise of protecting those liberties. Why should we be surprised?

The "communist threat" never lay within the Communist Party USA which, as *American Free Press* pointed out, was controlled at the highest levels by Morris Childs, an asset of J. Edgar Hoover's FBI: a Russian-born Zionist, Childs soured on Soviet-style communism when he detected the echoes of traditional Russian nationalism under Stalin. No, the Communist Party USA, was never a threat, although Hoover—a longtime ally of the Zionist Anti-Defamation League—was manipulating the tiny party for the covert agenda of his behind-the-scenes "advisors."

Nor did the communist threat lie even within the furthest "liberal" reaches of the Democratic Party. It was not the New Deal or the Fair Deal or Camelot or the Great Society—or Clintonism—that brought a unique updated American-style brand of Bolshevism of the Trotskyite bent to America. Instead, it was the "compassionate conservatism" of the man seriously being hailed as "the New Ronald Reagan": George W. Bush.

It is no coincidence that—just days into the war against Iraq—the "official" American organ of the Trotskyites—*Partisan Review*—closed its doors. In truth, the little intellectual journal now had no more reason to exist, for its aim of securing power had been accomplished through the proverbial "back door."

This book presents a brief but detailed overview of the intrigues of the neo-conservatives. Much more could be written, but it would perhaps belabor the point. Nonetheless, it seems appropriate to conclude, at this juncture, by saying quite simply:

It's Time to Declare War on the High Priests of War . . .

—MICHAEL COLLINS PIPER

EXECUTIVE SUMMARY:

THE HIGH PRIESTS OF WAR

The Secret History of How America's "Neo-Conservative" Trotskyites Came to Power and Orchestrated the War Against Iraq as the First Step in Their Drive for Global Empire

The report that follows is based on this foundation:

THAT the war against Iraq being waged by the American administration of President George W. Bush is not only contrary to traditional "conservative" American principles, but contrary to all principles of American foreign policy during the last half-century;

THAT the war against Iraq is being waged for far more broad-ranging purposes than "regime change" or "eliminating weapons of mass destruction"; first and foremost, as part of an overall effort to establish the United States as the sole international super-power, capable military and economically, to suppress any nations and/or peoples who dare to challenge American hegemony;

THAT the war against Iraq is simply a first step in a long-standing, wide-ranging plan to launch an even more aggressive move against the entire Arab Middle East in order to "remake the Arab world" to secure the survival of—and expand the power of—the state of Israel;

THAT the war against Iraq is only the initial target of this carefully planned scheme and that, ultimately, other Arab and Muslim states are slated for outright extinction or some form of occupation or control by American military and political forces (in alliance with Israel);

THAT the war against Iraq and the plan for the subjugation of the Arab people is quite simply a modified, modernized adaptation of the historic Zionist dream of "Greater Israel," adjusted to meet the demands of the international oil companies, which are, in turn, fully prepared to share the aim of dominating the oil-producing states of the Arab world in partnership with the state of Israel;

THAT the war against Iraq was deliberately orchestrated by a small but powerful network of hard-line "right wing" Zionist elements—the self-styled "neo-conservatives"—at the highest levels of the Bush administration, skillfully aided and abetted by like-minded persons in public policy organizations, think tanks, publications and other institutions, all of which are closely interconnected and, in turn, linked to hard-line "Likudnik" forces in Israel;

THAT the war against Iraq and the additional moves by the United States against the Arab world that are slated to follow can be traced to Zionist political intrigue inside the upper levels of the U.S. intelligence community, reaching as far back as the early 1970s, and that many of the same players involved in that activity are now guiding Bush administration policy today;

THAT the war against Iraq is an adjunct to the previously-declared "war against terrorism" which was, in itself, part of a long-evolving and carefully coordinated propaganda campaign founded on the theory that terrorism is somehow an "Arab" trait.

This report will examine all of these aspects, citing a wide variety of sources, and will focus largely on given facts that have received wide circulation in the "mainstream" English-language press in the United States.

The facts will speak for themselves. At any time this report delves into speculation or opinion, such views will be duly noted or otherwise clearly apparent.

—MCP

THE HIGH
PRIESTS
OF WAR

"If it were not for the strong support of the Jewish community for this war with Iraq, we would not be doing this. The leaders of the Jewish community are influential enough that they could change the direction of where this is going, and I think they should."

—U.S. Congressman Jim Moran (Democrat of Virginia) speaking at a public forum in his congressional district.[1]

Despite the very public frenzy in the United States that followed these remarks by liberal Congressman Jim Moran, even the influential New York-based Jewish newspaper, *Forward*, was forced to admit in its Feb. 28, 2003 issue that the role of the pro-Israel lobby and its adherents who held high-level policy-making positions in the administration of President George W. Bush were increasingly becoming a topic of public discussion. Congressman Moran had simply summarized the issue in a few short but controversial remarks.

Forward cited liberal American Jewish columnist Michael Kinsley who wrote on Oct. 24, 2002 that Israel's central role in the American debate over possible war with Iraq was "the proverbial elephant in the room." Of that elephant, Kinsley added: "Everybody sees it, no one mentions it." *Forward* stated it flatly: "Kinsley was referring to a debate, once only whispered in back rooms but lately splashed in bold characters across the mainstream media, over Jewish and Israeli influence in shaping American foreign policy."[2]

The Jewish newspaper noted that now, even "mainstream" American publications, ranging from *The Washington Post* to *The Economist* and even broadcast outlets such as CNN and MSNBC were featuring frank and open discussion of the topic. According to *Forward*'s assessment:

> Many of these articles project an image of President Bush and Prime Minister Sharon working in tandem to promote war against Iraq. Several of them described an administration packed with conservatives motivated primarily, if not solely, by a dedication to defending Israel.
>
> A few respected voices have even touched openly on the role of American Jewish organizations in the equation, suggesting a significant shift to the right on Middle East issues and an intense loyalty to Sharon. Still others raise the notion of Jewish and Israeli influence only to attack it as anti-Semitism.[3]

Yet, as if in confirmation of the basic thrust behind Congressman Moran's comments, even Ari Shavit, writing on April 9, 2003 in *Ha'aretz*, the Israeli newspaper, declared simply: "The war in Iraq was conceived by 25 neo-conservative intellectuals, most of them Jewish, who are pushing President Bush to change the course of history."[4]

In fact, as we will demonstrate, the historical record indicates—beyond question—that the then-impending war on Iraq was indeed largely the product of a long-standing—and carefully calculated and orchestrated—plan. That this plan aimed to establish an American global hegemony based upon the geopolitical aims of a small, but influential, group of policy makers inside the administration of President George W. Bush—a group tied intimately, for nearly a quarter of a century, to the grand design of a "Greater Israel," a longtime dream of the Zionist pioneers who founded the state of Israel and whose modern-day hawkish "right wing" followers are increasingly influential in all areas of Israeli society, particularly in the government realm.

This select group of Americans—now increasingly well known—describe themselves as the "neo-conservatives." They constitute a virtual "War Party" in America. They are unabashedly admiring and supportive of the hard-line Likud bloc in Israel led by Ariel Sharon. These neo-conservatives have directed policy decisions inside the Bush administration that have essentially placed the United States of America (under President

George W. Bush) in firm alliance with the Sharon regime in Israel.

The study we are about to undertake will provide a comprehensive overview of the history and development of the neo-conservative network, naming names and linking their policies to the elements in Israel with which they are allied.

But it is important to recognize that, in many respects, the policies that the neo-conservative "War Party" has been advancing are, from a historical standpoint, much at variance with the traditional American outlook. The policies of the "War Party" represent only a miniscule—albeit forceful and influential—faction in America. Philip Golub, a journalist and lecturer at the University of Paris VIII, has written of the neo-conservative strategy:

> The neo-conservative right has been attempting, with varying success, to establish itself as the dominant ideological force in the United States for more than 25 years, especially in the definition of foreign policy.
>
> Long thwarted by democratic process and public resistance to the national security state, it is now on the brink of success, thanks to George Bush's disputed electoral victory in 2000, and to 11 September 2001, which transformed an accidental president into an American Caesar. President Bush has become the neo-conservative vehicle for a policy that is based on unilateralism, permanent mobilisation and "preventive war."
>
> War and militarisation would have been impossible without 11 September, which tipped the institutional balance in favour of the new right. Apart from such opportunist motives as seizing the strategic chance to redraw the map of the Middle East and the Persian Gulf, this choice reflects much more far-reaching imperial ambitions . . .
>
> This authoritarian project became feasible in the unipolar world after 1991, when the US got a monopoly on the use of force in interstate relations. But it was conceived in the 1970s, when the extremist coalition now in control was first formed.
>
> The aim is to unite the nation and secure US strategic supremacy worldwide. The instruments are war and permanent mobilization, both requiring the constant identification of new enemies and the establishment of a strong national security state, which is independent of society.[5]

American author Michael Lind points out that the imperial dream outlined by the neo-conservative clique "was opposed by the mainstream U.S. foreign policy elite and by a majority of the American people, who according to polls opposed U.S. military action in Iraq and elsewhere without the support of allies and international institutions like the United Nations. The foreign policy of the radical right was enthusiastically supported by only two groups in the United States—neo-conservative policymakers and intellectuals at the elite level, and Southern Protestant voters within the mass voting public."[6]

Despite widespread opposition—both in the United States and across the globe—on March 17, 2003, American President George W. Bush formally announced that a war upon Iraq was imminent. After many long months of acrimonious debate, the American president declared that the United States—allied with Britain and a handful of countries—would effectively "go it alone," without the support of the world community.

Some critics would call to attention the fact that March 17 was the eve of Purim, the traditional Jewish holiday celebrating the victory by the ancient Jewish people over their hated enemy, Haman. However, not all Jews—in America or elsewhere—lined up with the "neo-conservative" clique, even though, in fact, most of the pivotal neo-conservative leaders are indeed Jewish.

RICHARD PERLE & WILLIAM KRISTOL

As American Jewish writer Stanley Heller pointed out in the days prior to the attack on Iraq: "We owe it to Americans to tell them the whole truth, that part of the war drive is being fueled by a wacko militarist clique from Israel and its interlocking bands of American Jewish and Christian supporters."[7] In addition, Professor Paul Gottfried—an American Jewish academic who calls himself a "conservative" but who objects strenuously to the activities of the self-styled "neo-conservatives"—added, writing elsewhere:

> No one who is sane is claiming that all Jews are collaborating with [neo-conservative pro-war leaders such as] Richard Perle and [William] Kristol. What is being correctly observed is a convergence of interests in which neo-conservatives have played a pivotal role. At this point they control almost all [Washington, D.C.] "conservative" think tanks, the "conservative" TV channel [pro-Zionist billionaire Rupert Murdoch's Fox News],*The Wall Street Journal, The New York Post*, and several major presses, together with just about every magazine that claims to be conservative.[8]

Professor Gottfried's comments thus introduce us to two key names that shall appear again and again in these pages: Richard Perle and William Kristol. They are perhaps the two most influential of the "War Party" neo-conservatives—by virtue of combined position, outreach and financial clout. They are the central players who have been responsible, in overwhelming part, for shaping the policies of the Bush administration that have led to the current conflict in the Middle East involving the deployment of American military forces against Iraq and the undeniably disastrous occupation which has followed.

Although we shall learn much more about Perle and Kristol, a brief introduction to the two neo-conservative figures is appropriate.

Often called "the Prince of Darkness," Richard Perle (who is Jewish) has been active in pro-Israel causes in official Washington since the mid-1970s when he was then an aide to powerful (now deceased) Sen. Henry M. Jackson (D-Washington), a leading congressional supporter of Israel. During that period, Perle was investigated on charges of espionage for Israel. Later Perle became a lobbyist for Israeli arms interests and eventually was appointed by President Ronald Reagan to a key post in the Department of Defense.

After leaving the Reagan administration, Perle remained active in Washington, DC, enmeshed in a wide variety of institutions and organizations, almost exclusively devoting his energies to advancing Israel's cause, and particularly that of the Likud Party of Ariel Sharon. Of recent date, Perle has maintained a special affiliation with the "neo-conservative" think tank known as the American Enterprise Institute.

However, when George W. Bush assumed the presidency, he named Perle to head the Defense Policy Board, a little-known but influential advisory board. It was from this post that Perle—utilizing his multiple contacts with longtime associates named to high posts inside the Bush administration itself—began making an active drive to advance the war against Iraq.

Although Perle resigned as chairman of the Defense Policy Board just days after the firing of the opening guns against Iraq—following allegations that he had conflicts of interest, stemming from his private financial business dealings that intersected with official government policies upon which he had an impact and from which he stood to personally benefit—he remained a member of the board, and certainly its most influential, until his formal resignation in March of 2004.

Considering all that we now know about Perle, it may be no coincidence that as far back as 1986 it was reported that once, while on a visit to Britain, Perle was introduced during a debate with then-Labor Party leader Denis Healey as "the person in charge of World War III."[9] Some Perle critics later suggested that the gentleman who made the remarks may have been empowered with psychic abilities, considering the critical role Perle has indeed played in sparking the American war against Iraq.

William Kristol (also Jewish) is equally influential, although in a different realm. As the son of an equally influential father, Irving Kristol—once described as the "godfather" of the neo-conservative movement—the younger Kristol parlayed his father's connections into a post as chief of staff to Vice President Dan Quayle who served under the first President Bush. But that was only Kristol's first step in his rise to vast power.

After the Bush-Quayle defeat by Bill Clinton in 1992, the younger Kristol, through his own aggressive efforts—not to mention increasingly favorable promotion of Kristol—by the major media, emerged as perhaps the best known voice of the "neo-conservative" philosophy. He became actively involved in setting up a well-funded and far-reaching public relations and information network, linked to numerous foundations and think tanks with which his father had already been associated.

In addition to accepting an appointment as editor of Rupert Murdoch's weekly national neo-conservative magazine, *The Weekly Standard*, Kristol also founded his own organization, Project for the New American Century.

As we shall see, Kristol's own operations and activities meshed precisely—actually, interlocked—with those of Richard Perle. And as the push for war against Iraq became increasingly more bellicose after George W. Bush became president—and then, even more so after the 9-11 terrorist attacks, which the neo-conservatives repeatedly sought to link to Iraqi leader Saddam Hussein—Perle and Kristol worked ever more closely, merging their own networks of influence to the point that the neo-conservative philosophy became the guiding force behind the entire Bush foreign policy making apparatus.

William Kristol—along with another close colleague, Robert

Kagan—has been the foremost publicist for the neo-conservative imperial strategy. Their book, released in the year 2000, *Present Dangers: Crisis and Opportunity in American Foreign and Defense Policy*, was a comprehensive statement of the neo-conservative point of view, featuring essays by Perle—of course—and an assembly of other neo-conservative "stars" associated with Kristol and Perle.

In a review of the book, former British diplomat Jonathan Clark commented that: "If the book's recommendations were implemented all at once, the U.S. would risk unilaterally fighting at least a five-front war, while simultaneously urging Israel to abandon the peace process in favour of a new no-holds-barred confrontation with the Palestinians."[10]

Ironically, as Michael Lind, a foremost critic of the neo-conservatives, has pointed out: "This turned out to be a prediction of the policies that the administration of George W. Bush would adopt in the following two years."[11] Lind notes: "The radical Zionist right to which [Perle and Kristol] belong is small in number but it has become a significant force in Republican policymaking circles."[12] Lind adds that the chief concern of many of those in this neo-conservative network is "the power and reputation of Israel."[13] He points out that they have waged vicious public relations campaigns against anyone who stands in their way—even including prominent and influential American military leaders who have questioned the neo-conservative policies.

THE ISRAELI CONNECTION

Thus, it is clear that the pro-Israel orientation of the neo-conservatives has been a primary matter of concern in the formulation (and conduct) of the policies they have sought to implement.

And this raises the question as to how much influence the state of Israel (and its American adherents, particularly in the neo-conservative network) did indeed play in sparking the war against Iraq.

As we have seen, the role of Israel in the Iraq affair was a problematic one in terms of protecting Israel (and American Jews) from a possible backlash by many Americans who resented the idea that perhaps U.S. policy was being predicated on the interests of Israel alone.

On November 27, 2002 *The Washington Post* reported that a group of

American political consultants who had previously advised Israeli politicians had been hired by the Israel Project—described as "a group funded by American Jewish organizations and individual donors"—to draft a memo to American Jewish leaders and Israeli leaders as to the best means by which to address the raging controversy over Iraq. The memo advised them: "If your goal is regime change, you must be much more careful with your language because of the potential backlash. You do not want Americans to believe that the war on Iraq is being waged to protect Israel rather than to protect America."[14] However, as Michael Lind reflected in his new biography of President Bush, the influence of Israel and the neoconservatives is undeniable:

> Under George W. Bush, the American executive branch and the government of Israel were fused in a degree without precedent in American history. . . . Bizarre as it seems, thanks to the influence of the Israeli model on neo-conservatives in the Bush administration, the United States, the leading power in the world, began acting as though it were an insecure and besieged international pariah state, like Israel under the leadership of the Likud Party.[15]

Writing in *Time* on Feb. 17, 2003, one of the most prominent of the American neo-conservatives in the media, columnist Charles Krauthammer, announced that the proposed war against Iraq "is not just to disarm Saddam. It is to reform a whole part of the world . . . What the U.S. needs in the Arab world is not an exit strategy but an entry strategy. Iraq is the beckoning door . . ." Krauthammer frankly named the targets of the neo-conservative war policy: "Iran, Saudi Arabia, Syria and beyond."[16]

In truth, published evidence indicates that the government of Israel did indeed desire a U.S. assault upon Iraq—as a first step toward additional action against other perceived enemies of the state of Israel. On February 18, 2003, the Israeli newspaper, *Ha'aretz*, reported that Israeli Prime Minister Ariel Sharon was calling for the United States to move on Iran, Libya and Syria after what was presumed to be the successful destruction of Iraq by the United States—a view no different than that expressed by the aforementioned Krauthammer.

Sharon said: "These are irresponsible states, which must be disarmed of weapons of mass destruction, and a successful American move in Iraq as a model will make that easier to achieve." The Israeli prime minister told a visiting delegation of American congressmen that "the American action [against Iraq] is of vital importance."[17]

The Israeli newspaper also reported that in meetings with Sharon and other Israeli officials, U.S. Undersecretary of State John Bolton—one of the key "neo-conservatives" inside the Bush administration who had been promoting war against Iraq—had said, in the Israeli newspaper's words, that Bolton felt that after Iraq had been dealt with "it would be necessary thereafter to deal with threats from Syria, Iran and North Korea."[18]

In addition, on Feb. 27, 2003, *The New York Times* freely reported that Israel not only advocated a U.S. war on Iraq but that Israel also believed that, ultimately, the war should be expanded to other nations perceived to be threats to Israel. The *Times* stated:

> Many in Israel are so certain of the rightness of a war on Iraq that officials are already thinking past that conflict to urge a continued, assertive American role in the Middle East. Defense Minister Shaul Mofaz told members of the Conference of Presidents of Major American Jewish Organizations last week that after Iraq, the United States should generate "political, economic, diplomatic pressure" on Iran. "We have great interest in shaping the Middle East the day after" a war, he said. Israel regards Iran and Syria as greater threats and is hoping that once Saddam Hussein is dispensed with, the dominoes will start to tumble.[19]

And while there were American Jews, acting independently of the established Jewish community leadership organizations, who opposed the war against Iraq, there is no question that elite American Jewish organizations closely tied to Israeli intelligence and the government of Israel were firmly behind the drive for war. Those organizations were acting as Jewish organizations, purporting to represent all Jewish Americans when in fact they did not.

After the war erupted, the Anti-Defamation League (ADL) of B'nai B'rith—described by critics as a propaganda arm of Israel's clandestine services, the Mossad—issued a statement. It declared: "We express our support for the United States Government in its effort to stop Iraqi President Saddam Hussein and the danger he poses to the stability and safety of the region. The need to stop Saddam Hussein is clear."[20]

CRITICS RISE UP IN AMERICA

However, while the Israeli leadership and their neo-conservative allies were calling for war, there were many Americans of all races, creeds and colors who were standing up and declaring their opposition.

In the months of debate leading up to the American attack on Iraq, Rep. Dennis Kucinich (D-Ohio) emerged as perhaps the most outspoken and articulate congressional critic of the proposed war. He sounded out multiple arguments against the war, ruling it totally unfounded and counter to all traditional American policy:

> Unilateral military action by the United States against Iraq is unjustified, unwarranted, and illegal. . . .
>
> Unilateral action on the part of the United States, or in partnership with Great Britain, would for the first time set our nation on the bloodstained path of aggressive war, a sacrilege upon the memory of those who fought to defend this country. America's moral authority would be undermined throughout the world. It would destabilize the entire Persian Gulf and Middle East region . . .
>
> Policies of aggression are not worthy of any nation with a democratic tradition, let alone a nation of people who love liberty and whose sons and daughters sacrifice to maintain that democracy.
>
> The question is not whether or not America has the military power to destroy Saddam Hussein and Iraq. The question is whether we destroy something essential in this nation by asserting that America has the right to do so anytime it pleases.
>
> America cannot and should not be the world's policeman. America cannot and should not try to pick the leaders of other nations. Nor should America and the American people be pressed into the service of international oil interests and arms dealers . . .
>
> If the United States proceeds with a first strike policy, then we will have taken upon our nation a historic burden of committing a violation of international law, and we would then forfeit any moral high ground we could hope to hold.[21]

Quite remarkably, even after the war actually began, Kucinich refused to be silent, refusing to be bullied into supporting the war under the guise of "supporting the troops"—a popular catchphrase that has historically been used to convince Americans to support an unpopular war after American troops have been formally committed to action. Undaunted by accusations of being "unpatriotic," etc, Kucinich said:

> I support the troops. But, this war is illegal and wrong. I do not support this
> mission. I will not vote to fund this Administration's war in Iraq. This war is
> killing our troops. This war is killing innocent Iraqi civilians. This war must end
> now. It was unjust when it started two weeks ago, and is still unjust today. The
> U.S. should get out now and try to save the lives of American troops and Iraqi
> citizens. Ending the war now and resuming weapons inspections could salvage
> world opinion of the United States. The greatest threat to the United States at this
> time is terrorism, which this war will breed.[22]

Kucinich was not the only American public official to take a daring
public stand against the war—but he was certainly one of the most forthright and outspoken.

Just as American troops began their assault on the Arab republic, the
longest serving member of the U.S. Senate—and the former leader of the
Senate Democrats—Sen. Robert Byrd of West Virginia delivered a blis-
tering address on the Senate floor, declaring the war to be totally at odds
with traditional American policy. He said, in part:

> Today I weep for my country. I have watched the events of recent months
> with a heavy, heavy heart. No more is the image of America one of strong, yet
> benevolent peacekeeper.
>
> We proclaim a new doctrine of preemption which is understood by few and
> feared by many. We say that the United States has the right to turn its firepower
> on any corner of the globe which might be suspect in the war on terrorism. We
> assert that right without the sanction of any international body. As a result, the
> world has become a much more dangerous place. We flaunt our superpower sta-
> tus with arrogance.
>
> When did we become a nation which ignores and berates our friends? When
> did we decide to risk undermining international order by adopting a radical and
> doctrinaire approach to using our awesome military might? How can we aban-
> don diplomatic efforts when the turmoil in the world cries out for diplomacy?[23]

Clearly, although the neo-conservatives hardly reflected the thinking
of many Americans of many political persuasions, they did indeed reflect
a particular brand of philosophy and one indubitably bound up with the
hard-line imperial agenda of Israel's Likud.

And with that in mind, it is appropriate to begin examining the nature
of the neo-conservative network that rules the roost in official Washington
under the administration of George W. Bush.

THE NEO-CONSERVATIVE NETWORK

On December 13, 2002, *Counterpunch* magazine, published by maverick Irish-born American-based journalist Alexander Cockburn, featured an article raising the questions of "the Bush administration's dual loyalties" and provided a fascinating overview of the neo-conservative network that ultimately led America to war. The authors were Bill and Kathleen Christison, a husband-and-wife team of former veteran U.S. Central Intelligence Agency analysts. They cited the Israeli sympathies of top neo-conservative policy makers inside the Bush administration, pointing out that—indeed—these neo-conservatives were closely aligned with the ideology of the Likud bloc in Israel. Their summary of the "cast of characters" among the neo-conservatives is precise and worth noting:

> Deputy Secretary of Defense Paul Wolfowitz leads the pack. He was a protégé of Richard Perle, who heads the prominent Pentagon advisory body, the Defense Policy Board. Many of today's neo-conservatives, including Perle, are the intellectual progeny of the late Senator Henry "Scoop" Jackson, a strong defense hawk and one of Israel's most strident congressional supporters in the 1970s.
>
> Wolfowitz in turn is the mentor of Lewis "Scooter" Libby, now Vice President Cheney's chief of staff who was first a student of Wolfowitz and later a subordinate during the 1980s in both the State and the Defense Departments.
>
> Another Perle protégé is Douglas Feith, who is currently undersecretary of defense for policy, the department's number-three man, and has worked closely with Perle both as a lobbyist for Turkey and in co-authoring strategy papers for right-wing Israeli governments.
>
> Assistant Secretaries Peter Rodman and Dov Zakheim, old hands from the Reagan administration when the neo-cons first flourished, fill out the subcabinet ranks at Defense. At lower levels, the Israel and the Syria/Lebanon desk officers at Defense are imports from the Washington Institute for Near East Policy, a think tank spun off from the pro-Israel lobby organization, AIPAC.
>
> Neo-conservatives have not made many inroads at the State Department, except for John Bolton, an American Enterprise Institute hawk and Israeli proponent who is said to have been forced on a reluctant Colin Powell as undersecretary for arms control. Bolton's special assistant is David Wurmser, who wrote and/or co-authored with Perle and Feith at least two strategy papers for Israeli Prime Minister Netanyahu in 1996.
>
> Wurmser's wife, Meyrav Wurmser, is a co-founder of the media-watch web-

site MEMRI (Middle East Media Research Institute), which is run by retired Israeli military and intelligence officers and specializes in translating and widely circulating Arab media and statements by Arab leaders. A recent investigation by *The Guardian* of London found that MEMRI's translations are skewed by being highly selective. Although it inevitably translates and circulates the most extreme of Arab statements, it ignores moderate Arab commentary and extremist Hebrew statements.

In the vice president's office, Cheney has established his own personal national security staff, run by aides known to be very pro-Israel. The deputy director of the staff, John Hannah, is a former fellow of the Israeli-oriented Washington Institute.

On the National Security Council staff, the newly appointed director of Middle East affairs is Elliott Abrams, who came to prominence after pleading guilty to withholding information from Congress during the Iran-contra scandal (and was pardoned by President Bush the elder) and who has long been a vocal proponent of right-wing Israeli positions. Putting him in a key policymaking position on the Palestinian-Israeli conflict is like entrusting the henhouse to a fox.

Probably the most important organization, in terms of its influence on Bush administration policy formulation, is the Jewish Institute for National Security Affairs (JINSA). Formed after the 1973 Arab-Israeli war specifically to bring Israel's security concerns to the attention of U.S. policymakers and concentrating also on broad defense issues, the extremely hawkish, right-wing JINSA has always had a high-powered board able to place its members inside conservative U.S. administrations. Cheney, Bolton, and Feith were members until they entered the Bush administration. Several lower level JINSA functionaries are now working in the Defense Department.

Wolfowitz himself has been circumspect in public, writing primarily about broader strategic issues rather than about Israel specifically or even the Middle East, but it is clear that at bottom Israel is a major interest and may be the principal reason for his near obsession with the effort, of which he is the primary spearhead, to dump Saddam Hussein, remake the Iraqi government in an American image, and then further redraw the Middle East map by accomplishing the same goals in Syria, Iran, and perhaps other countries.

But his interest in Israel always crops up. Even profiles that downplay his attachment to Israel nonetheless always mention the influence the Holocaust, in which several of his family perished, has had on his thinking. One source inside the administration has described him frankly as "over-the-top crazy when it comes to Israel." Although this probably accurately describes most of the rest of the neo-con coterie, and Wolfowitz is guilty at least by association, he is actually more complex and nuanced than this.[24]

The Christisons pointed out that a *New York Times Magazine* profile of Wolfowitz by the *Times'* Bill Keller cites critics who say that "Israel exercises a powerful gravitational pull on the man"[25] and notes that as a teenager Wolfowitz lived in Israel during his mathematician father's sabbatical semester there. In addition, his sister is married to an Israeli. Keller even somewhat reluctantly acknowledges the accuracy of one characterization of Wolfowitz as "Israel-centric." However, the Christisons note, "Keller goes through considerable contortions to shun what he calls 'the offensive suggestion of dual loyalty' and in the process makes one wonder if he is protesting too much."[26]

So the facts about the neo-conservative clique governing Bush administration policies are very clear. However, much of the mainstream media in America initially hesitated to emphasize the remarkable linkage and longtime associations of this clique of like-minded political power brokers. The independent media in America—such as the Washington-based *American Free Press*, among the foremost—that did dare to mention the prominent role of the "neo-cons" were often attacked as "conspiracy theorists" and even as "anti-Semites," among many similar terms often used to confuse the issue and thereby redirect attention away from the intrigues of Israel and its American lobby.

THE TRUTH EMERGES IN THE US MEDIA

Nonetheless, once the long-planned "neo-conservative"-orchestrated war against Iraq was safely under way, a front-page article in the March 21, 2003 issue of the pro-war *Wall Street Journal* admitted the truth. The headline in the article was straightforward: "A New Mideast—President's Dream: Changing Not Just Regime but a Region. A Pro-U.S., Democratic Area Is a Goal That Has Israeli and Neo-Conservative Roots." The article began by declaring frankly: "As he sends American troops and planes into Iraq, President Bush has in mind more than changing a country. His dream is make the entire Middle East a different place, and one safer for American interests."[27]

The article proceeded to describe the power of the pro-war neo-conservative network surrounding Richard Perle and his collaborator, William Kristol. The article summarized the events leading up to the decision by President Bush to wage war against Iraq and the role of the neo-conservatives in that process.

Just three days later, on March 24, 2003, the *New York Times* published a similar overview, declaring that the doctrine of preemptive war advocated by the neo-conservatives had its roots in the early 1990s. (However, as we shall see, the overall neo-conservative agenda goes back much further than that.) The *Times* article cited an un-named administration official as saying of the Iraq war: "This is just the beginning."[28]

THE EX-COMMUNISTS BECOME NEO-CONSERVATIVES

To understand the political orientation of the "neo-conservatives" and their agenda, it is critical to recognize not only the important role played today by the aforementioned William Kristol but also that of his father and mother and their associates who are central to the story of the development of the neo-conservative power bloc in America.

Although today Kristol is perhaps the best known of the neo-conservative voices in the media, he is much more than that. Not only is the chief public relations strategist—some might say "propagandist"—for the neo-conservatives, but he is also the scion of a powerful husband-and-wife team of American Jewish writers—self-described "ex-Trotskyites"—Irving Kristol and Gertrude Himmelfarb. The senior Kristol—along with a handful of other like-minded thinkers—is generally hailed as the primary founding force behind the neo-conservative movement.

According to the American Jewish weekly, *Forward*, the small "mostly Jewish"[29] group of "New York Intellectuals"[30] operating in the senior Kristol's sphere of influence were "known to insiders as "The Family.""[31]—a designation that suggests to those schooled in the intrigues of the Cold War, perhaps some cryptic, almost cult-like bond, even a classic communist "cell."

And indeed, there is a Cold War connection to Kristol and "The Family," for—during the period from the 1930s to the 1950s—they were disciples of Leon Trotsky, the Bolshevik revolutionary, and arch critics of Trotsky's fierce rival, Josef Stalin, who emerged as leader of the Soviet Union after forcing Trotsky into exile. However, as years passed, starting

in the late 1950s and especially in the 1960s, their political philosophy
began, it is said, to "evolve." Yet, there are those who would say that the
ex-Trotskyites are anything but "ex" at all; that, instead, they remain tried
and true Trotskyites who have adapted their traditional philosophy to
modern concerns, events, and political realities.

Michael Lind, author of a new biography of President George W.
Bush, has noted the origins of this tightly-knit core then surrounding
Kristol and in years to come and explains their shift in viewpoint:

> Neo-conservatives were not traditional conservative Republicans. Most had
> been liberal or leftist Democrats; some had originally been Marxists. Many were
> Jewish and had broken with the Democratic left because of leftist hostility to
> Israel's occupation of Arab land after 1967 and the hostility of many Black
> Power militants to both Jewish-Americans and Israel. Ronald Reagan was the
> first Republican president that many neo-conservatives had voted for.
>
> While the foreign policy of the traditional Republican establishment reflect-
> ed the fear of international disorder of the business elite, neo-conservative strat-
> egy reflected the crusading ideological fervor of former Wilsonian liberals [refer-
> ring to former American President Woodrow Wilson who was a proponent of
> American interventionism abroad] and former Marxist revolutionaries, com-
> bined, in the case of many Jewish neo-conservatives, with an emotional ethnic
> commitment to the well-being of Israel.[32]

ISRAEL AND THE NEO-CONSERVATIVES

American Jewish scholar, Benjamin Ginsberg, has described the central role of Israel's security in the thinking of the neo-conservatives and
on their political activities during the last quarter of the 20th century:

> Neo-conservative Jewish intellectuals were instrumental during the 1970s and
> 1980s in developing justifications for increased defense spending, as well as linking
> American military aid to Israel to the more general American effort to contain the
> Soviet Union.
>
> Israel was portrayed as an American "strategic asset" that could play an impor-
> tant role in containing Soviet expansion into the Middle East.
>
> A number of Jewish neo-conservatives became active in [lobbying] for increased
> levels of defense spending and the strengthening of America's defense capabilities
> against what they asserted was a heightened threat of Soviet expansionism.[33]

A similar, although less friendly, assessment of the neo-conservatives was put forth in 1986 by famed American novelist Gore Vidal. Responding to allegations that he (Vidal) was "anti-Semitic" because of his criticism of the unusual degree to which American Jewish "neo-conservatives" were attached to Israel—more so than to America—Vidal called the neo-conservatives "empire lovers" and charged that there was one reason why these ex-Trotskyites were now so enamored of American military power:

> In order to get [United States] Treasury money for Israel (last year $3 billion), pro-Israel lobbyists must see to it that America's "the Russians are coming" squads are in place so that they can continue to frighten the American people into spending enormous sums for "defense," which also means the support of Israel in its never-ending wars against just about everyone. To make sure that nearly a third of the Federal budget goes to the Pentagon and Israel, it is necessary for the pro-Israel lobbyists to make common cause with our lunatic right.[34]

At the time, however, Vidal had no idea how powerful the neo-conservatives would ultimately become. But, Vidal remains an outspoken critic of U.S. and Israeli imperialism, and is one of the most highly regarded English-language novelists in the world today.

Whatever their recognition among "intellectual" circles, the "neo-conservative" elements were virtual strangers (and still remain so) to the broad audience of American citizens. In fact, probably the first time the term "neo-conservative" was introduced to a wide-ranging national American audience was in the Nov. 7, 1977 issue of *Newsweek*, published by the same company that publishes *The Washington Post* newspaper.

By 1979, the first full-length book study of the "neo-conservatives" was issued by author Peter Steinfels. Entitled *The Neo-Conservatives: The Men Who Are Changing America's Politics*, this book described neo-conservatism as "a distinct and powerful political outlook [that had] recently emerged in the United States."[35]

The author hailed Irving Kristol, father of William Kristol, as "the standard bearer of neo-conservatism"[36] and focused largely on Kristol and fellow intellectuals who were shaping the neo-conservative point of view.

The book painted neo-conservatism as a newly-developing philosophy and largely focused on its domestic political outlook. Remarkably, very little of the book was even devoted to the neo-conservative foreign policy agenda, despite the fact that the neo-conservatives were, from the beginning, heavily focused on foreign policy. However, Steinfels did note that the neo-conservatives were, quite naturally, as ex-Trotskyites, hostile to the Soviet Union of Josef Stalin and his legacy.

However, the author did note the fact that there were many rumors swirling around Kristol, specifically the allegation that as far back as the 1950s, Kristol had been receiving subsidies from the American Central Intelligence Agency (CIA).

THE CIA AND THE NEO-CONSERVATIVES

In fact, as a far more recent volume, *The Cultural Cold War: The CIA and the World of Arts and Letters,* by Frances Stonor Saunders reveals, the circles in which Kristol was a key player—surrounding a group known as the Congress for Cultural Freedom (which existed from 1950 to 1967) and the American Committee for Cultural Freedom (which existed from 1950 to 1957)—were indeed funded by the CIA. The author exhaustively investigated the activities of Kristol and his associates and has confirmed that Kristol owed much of his early fame and publicity to support from American intelligence.[37]

According to a 1986 study by Sidney Blumenthal, a Jewish-American reporter for *The Washington Post* who later became a top advisor to President Bill Clinton, Irving Kristol was known as "the Godfather" of the neo-conservative movement to whom others went seeking sinecures and funding. Kristol "could arrange offers from institutes and foundations [so lucrative] that no conservative would refuse."

One of Kristol's protégés, Jude Wanniski—who has since largely broken with the "neo-cons"—was quoted as describing Kristol as "the invisible hand" behind the neo-conservative movement.[38] Blumenthal noted that Kristol's power was such that it could be compared to "a circuitry of influence that blinks like a Christmas tree when he plugs in."[39] In fact, through his magazines, *The National Interest* and *The Public Interest*, Kristol has expanded his influence, not only within Republican Party ranks but within the public arena as a whole.

Noting the Trotskyite origins of the "neo-conservatives," Sidney Blumenthal assessed the nature of the "neo-conservative" migration into—some might say "invasion of—the Republican Party, saying: "The neo-conservatives are the Trotskyites of Reaganism, and Kristol is a Trotskyite transmuted into a man of the right."[40]

All of this having been noted for the record, the fact is that today, William Kristol—son of neo-conservative "godfather" Irving Kristol—is carrying on the family's legacy, one that reaches back to the internecine philosophical struggles of the Bolshevik era and the Cold War between the United States and the Soviet Union that followed. The younger Kristol is, beyond any question, in his own right, one of the most powerful opinion-makers on the face of the planet today.

THE MURDOCH CONNECTION

Acting as a self-appointed "conservative leader," Kristol, whom, as we have noted, is publisher and editor of billionaire Rupert Murdoch's *Weekly Standard* magazine, has consistently called for U.S. intervention abroad, particularly as a means to advance the interests of the state of Israel—a stand congruent with Murdoch's own known sympathies for the hard-line Likud bloc in Israel. (Murdoch himself is of partial Jewish descent, from his mother's side, although this detail has often gone unmentioned in even "mainstream" accounts citing Murdoch's infatuation with the Zionist cause.)

Over the years a variety of critics have alleged that Kristol's sponsor, Murdoch, is essentially a long-time media representative—a highly-paid "front man"—for the combined forces of the Rothschild, Bronfman and Oppenheimer families who, with Murdoch, were referred to by critics as far back as the early 1980s as "The Billionaire Gang of Four."

This clique of billionaires are tied together not only by a mutual association in international financial affairs but also by their Jewish heritage and a devotion to promoting the interests of the state of Israel. They are also widening their control and influence over the American media with Murdoch's operations being perhaps the most public.

KRISTOL'S MEN IN THE BUSH WHITE HOUSE

In fact, Kristol's personal tentacles inside all reaches of the Bush administration are immense. On March 19, 2002 *The Washington Post* described Kristol's wide-ranging and intimate ties to key White House insiders. Noting that one Joseph Shattan had been hired as a speechwriter for the president, the *Post* added, pointedly:

> Shattan, who worked for Kristol when he was Vice President Dan Quayle's chief of staff, will join Bush speechwriter Matthew Scully and [Vice President] Cheney speechwriter John McConnell, both of whom also worked under Kristol on the Quayle staff. Fellow Bush speechwriter Peter Wehner worked for Kristol when he was chief of staff to then-Education Secretary William Bennett [himself a protégé of Kristol's father, Irving Kristol], while National Security Council speechwriter Matthew Rees worked for Kristol at *The Weekly Standard*.[41]

In effect, many of the very persons writing the official speeches and public statements for not only the president and the vice president, but also other key foreign policy makers, owed their patronage to Kristol. However, the *Post* noted, Kristol's influence, went beyond that. Others inside the Bush administration also owed their loyalty to Kristol:

> Energy Secretary Spencer Abraham is a Kristol acolyte from the Quayle days while drug control policy chief John Walters worked under Kristol at the Education Department. Jay Lefkowitz, the new director of Bush's Domestic Policy Council, was Kristol's lawyer. Other Kristol pals include National Security Council Director Elliott Abrams, Cheney Chief of Staff I. Lewis "Scooter" Libby, Deputy Defense Secretary Paul Wolfowitz, Undersecretary of State John Bolton and Leon Kass, the head of Bush's bioethics panel. The tentacles reach into [Bush's personal inner circle]: Al Hubbard, a close Bush friend, was Kristol's deputy on the Quayle staff.[42]

What makes all of this so particularly remarkable is that Kristol himself backed Bush's Republican primary opponent, Arizona Sen. John McCain, a feverish supporter of Israel, in the 2000 presidential campaign. As such, it might be said, Kristol—initially, perhaps, somewhat of an "outsider" in Bush circles—very much became an "insider"—and one with incredible and un-rivaled influence.

One of Kristol's critics noted the massive promotion that Kristol received in the American media, commenting as early as 1996 that Kristol was, "by quite some distance, the most widely quoted private citizen in the media [and, as a consequence] the most important strategist in the Republican Party."[43]

What this means, essentially, is that when the major American media wanted to promote a particular idea or viewpoint, newspaper reporters and broadcast journalists turned to Kristol for his "neo-conservative" point of view—often to the exclusion of better-known, more respected, and more knowledgeable individuals. Some say that this is no coincidence, considering what is perceived to be a strong pro-Israel bias on the part of the major media.

With William Kristol acting as an articulate and forceful media functionary, the "neo-conservative" forces inside the Bush administration have had a powerful ally who, in turn, has extremely lucrative resources—and international connections of influence—supporting him.

As such, in the wake of the 9-11 terrorist attacks, when the Bush administration geared up to respond to the assault on America, Kristol and his neo-conservative forces began rallying to broaden the U.S. response against the prime suspect, Islamic fundamentalist leader Osama bin Laden, into an all-out assault on the Arab and Muslim worlds.

Initially, Secretary of State Colin Powell seemed to be the one well-known figure in the Bush administration who stood in the way of an American imperial policy hinging on a war against Iraq.

Joined by the military's Joint Chiefs of Staff in urging a cautious approach to the crisis, Powell was being confronted inside the Bush administration by a tightly-knit group of hard-driving warmongers trying to run roughshod over the administration's stated policy and determined to subvert it for their own ends.

While Deputy Secretary of Defense Paul Wolfowitz was the Israeli lobby's key point man inside the Bush administration pushing for an all-out assault on key Arab states such as Iraq and Syria—not to mention the Islamic Republic of Iran—his efforts were being ably promoted by the efforts of William Kristol and his "neo-conservative" political and propaganda network.

KISSINGER AND KRISTOL

In its Sept. 24, 2001 issue, the Washington-based *American Free Press* gave a capsule summary of Kristol's background, noting that he is a member of the secretive Bilderberg group, funded jointly by the Rockefeller and Rothschild financial empires. Kristol is also a member of the Council on Foreign Relations, which is perhaps "the" elite American policy making group—the American affiliate of the Rothschild-funded London-based Royal Institute of International Affairs.

An investigation by the *American Free Press* uncovered further details about the Kristol family's wide-ranging contacts. With former Secretary of State Henry Kissinger serving on their board of directors, the Kristols operate a company known as National Affairs, Inc., which issues two publications, *The National Interest* and *The Public Interest*.

Much of their company's funding comes from the Lynde and Harry Bradley Foundation, with which the younger Kristol was previously associated. In fact, this foundation—as we'll see further—is known for its generous funding of anti-Arab and anti-Islamic propaganda causes.

While, as noted, Irving Kristol has long been a key player inside the influential "neo-conservative" American Enterprise Institute, his son William Kristol maintained at least two other primary public relations outlets of his own:

1) Empower America, co-founded by Kristol with two former Congressmen, Jack Kemp (R-N.Y.) and Vin Weber (R-Minn.), and former Education Secretary William Bennett—three non-Jews, incidentally—all known for their enthusiastic and loudly and often stated devotion to the pro-Israel cause; and

2) Kristol's more recent venture, the newly-formed Project for the New American Century, an unabashedly internationalist pressure group calling for the exercise of American military might abroad, particularly in pursuit of measures designed to advance the interests of Israel.

Just one week after the 9-11 terrorist attack on the United States—in conjunction with neo-conservative Deputy Defense Secretary Paul Wolfowitz's campaign inside the Bush administration to broaden the war against terrorism to include efforts to crush Arab and Islamic states that are perceived by Israel to be its enemies—William Kristol issued a call to arms signed by a host of foreign policy luminaries, echoing Wolfowitz. These luminaries, in turn, used their connections through the academic, media and policy-making establishments to pressure the Bush adminis- tration for the action Wolfowitz demanded.

THE TANGLED WEB OF RICHARD PERLE

Most influential among Kristol's collaborators who signed that letter is the ubiquitous Richard Perle, the former Reagan era assistant secretary of defense for international security policy. In fact, Perle is perhaps the singular driving force behind a closely-knit group (including Wolfowitz) whose origins in the modern-day national security establishment go back to the 1970s when Perle was a top aide to the late Sen. Henry M. Jackson (D-Wash.).

Perle and one of his closest collaborators, Stephen J. Bryen, first appeared on the Washington scene as highly influential U.S. Senate staffers. Perle was a top aide to then-Sen. Jackson, chairman of the piv- otal Senate Armed Services Committee. Bryen was a senior aide to then- Sen. Clifford Case (R-N.J.), a high-ranking GOP member of the Senate Foreign Relations Committee.

Both Jackson and Case were known as ardent public advocates for Israel. But behind the scenes, their two assistants were busy providing "special services" to the tiny, yet powerful, Middle East state.

In 1970, after the National Security Council ordered a wiretap of the Israeli Embassy in Washington, Perle was revealed to be passing classi- fied information to an officer of the Israeli embassy. Although then-CIA Director Stansfield Turner angrily demanded that Jackson fire Perle, Jackson refused, lending fuel to the fire of long-standing speculation that the Israeli lobby had a "hold" over the veteran lawmaker.

By 1975 Jewish-American journalist Stephen Isaacs, a writer for *The Washington Post*, was noting in his book, *Jews and American Politics*, that Perle—along with another top Jewish congressional staff member, Morris Amitay, who later headed the American Israel Public Affairs Committee, or AIPAC, a top lobby for Israel—"command[ed] a tiny army of Semitophiles on Capitol Hill and direct Jewish power in behalf of Jewish interests."[44]

THE TEAM B AFFAIR

But Perle's influence reached far beyond the halls of Congress. Not only was he a key "inside" player on behalf of the Israeli lobby on Capitol Hill, but during the mid-1970s he also played a critical part in the selection of a formal body—officially known as "Team B"—that functioned as a purportedly "independent" advisory council on intelligence estimates relating to Soviet aims and capabilities.

In fact, the members of Team B were bound by their determination to make every aspect of U.S. foreign policy geared toward policies that would prove beneficial to Israel.

To understand what is happening in our world today as a consequence of the rule of the neo-conservatives in official Washington, it is critical to understand the geopolitical events surrounding the history of the group known as Team B.

Although Team B was debated and discussed at the highest levels, it was not until the late Andrew St. George, an eminent international correspondent, formerly associated with *Life* magazine, began writing about its history in the pages of a maverick national weekly newspaper *The Spotlight*, that the story of Team B reached a widespread audience.

Team B emerged in the mid-1970s at which time hawkish factions in the Israeli government were lobbying hard in Washington for more arms aid and cash infusions through the U.S. foreign aid program. Loyal supporters of Israel such as Sen. Jackson argued that Israel needed more military might to protect the Middle East against "Soviet aggression"—an argument that delighted hard-line anti-communists in both political parties. Israel was playing the "Soviet card" to the utmost.

The Israelis were arguing vehemently against détente for they feared that cooperation between the United States and the Soviet Union could result in joint actions by the two super-powers that could prove inimical to Israeli interests.

As such, it was in 1974 that University of Chicago Professor Albert Wohlstetter accused the CIA of systematically underestimating Soviet missile deployment. Wohlstetter—a widely known architect of U.S. nuclear strategy—also happened to be Richard Perle's longtime intellectual mentor.[45] In fact, the relationship was even closer: growing up in Los

Angeles, Perle was a high school friend of Wohlstetter's daughter.

Based largely on Wohlstetter's opening gun, Perle and other pro-Israel activists on Capitol Hill and in official Washington began attacking the CIA and demanding additional inquiry into the CIA's analysis of Soviet strength. Perle used the offices of Sen. Jackson—who was angling for the Democratic Party's presidential nomination in 1976, primarily financed by American Jewish backers—as the "headquarters" for the attack on the CIA.

However, U.S. intelligence analysts were scoffing at Israel's alarmist cries. Led by senior analysts in the Office of National Estimates, they reassured the White House that, at least for the moment, the Soviets had neither the intent nor the capability to attack a major target of vital U.S. interest, such as the oil-rich Gulf states.

Nonetheless, Israel's Washington allies maneuvered in an effort to counter-balance the findings of the Office of National Estimates. Under political pressure from Senator Jackson and other supporters of Israel, President Gerald Ford agreed in mid-1976 (while George Bush was serving as CIA director) to institute a so-called "audit" of intelligence data provided by the CIA's own National Intelligence Officers (soon to be called the "A-Team"] by a committee of "independent" experts—known as the "B-Team."

However, the newly-established and ostensibly "independent" group—B-Team—headed by Harvard professor Richard Pipes, a Russian-born devotee of the Zionist cause, became an outpost of Israeli influence.

(Years later Pipes' son, Daniel Pipes, would emerge as one of the neo-conservative network's leading anti-Arab and anti-Muslim propagandists, operating a well-funded think tank, the Middle East Institute—operating closely with Perle. In the summer of 2003, President George W. Bush named the younger Pipes to the federally-sponsored U.S. Peace Institute, despite the widespread objections of many persons who viewed Pipes to be a bigoted hate-monger with a single-minded political agenda.)

In any case, Richard Perle was largely responsible for the selection of the Team B membership. Paul Wolfowitz was among those selected for Team B because of Perle's recommendation. Likewise with veteran diplomat Paul Nitze, among other prominent members of the team selected.

Anne Hessing Cahn, a later student of the Team B affair, has written that "There was an almost incestuous closeness among most of the B Team members,"[46] quoting Perle as saying, that "The Jewish neo-conservative connection sprang from that period of worries about detente and Israel."[47] Robert Bowie, former CIA deputy director for national intelligence, described the efforts of Team B as "a fight for the soul of the Republican party, for getting control of foreign policy within one branch of the party."[48]

In the meantime, John Paisley, recently retired from the CIA, was appointed by CIA Director Bush to act as the CIA's liaison between the CIA's own in-house "Team A" and the Israeli-influenced "Team B." Meade Rowington, a former U.S. counterintelligence analyst quoted by Andrew St. George in *The Spotlight* on Feb. 5, 1996 noted: "It soon became clear to Paisley that these cosmopolitan intellectuals were simply trying to discredit the CIA's recommendations and replace them with the alarmist view of Soviet intentions favored by Israeli estimators."[49]

By early 1978 the B-Team had finished its review of the CIA's procedures and programs and issued a lengthy report that was harshly critical of almost every finding U.S. intelligence had made in previous years about Soviet military power and its intended uses.

The Israeli-influenced B-Team report said that the Soviets were secretly developing a so-called "first-strike" capability, because Soviet strategic doctrine assumed that such a sneak attack would make them the winners of a nuclear exchange with the United States. The B-Team dismissed the estimates of analysts who held that Moscow was unlikely to start a nuclear conflict unless attacked. In the end, of course, the B-Team findings prevailed and the direct consequence was that there was a virtual revival of the arms race and a massive new infusion of U.S. military and other aid to Israel during the 1980s.

Drawing on what critics charged (and which proved to be) fraudulent estimates provided by Israeli intelligence—the foundation of the B-Team's report was the warning that the Soviet Union was fast running out of its petroleum supplies.

As a consequence, the B-Team forecast that beginning in 1980 Soviet oil production would suffer critical shortfalls, forcing Moscow to import as much as 4.5 million barrels a day for its essential needs. Starved for oil—the Israeli disinformation claimed—the Soviets would invade Iran or another oil-rich Gulf state even if it meant a nuclear confrontation with the United States.

Although the team's final report was secret, with access reserved for a handful of government leaders, John Paisley reportedly got his hands on a copy of the report in the summer of 1978 and set to work writing a detailed critique that would destroy this Israeli disinformation. But Paisley was murdered before he could ever complete his task.

According to Richard Clement, who headed the Interagency Committee on Counter-Terrorism during the Reagan administration: "The Israelis had no compunction about 'terminating' key American intelligence officials who threatened to blow the whistle on them. Those of us familiar with the case of Paisley know that he was killed by the Mossad. But no one, not even in Congress, wants to stand up and say so publicly."[50]

Solid evidence compiled over the years by a variety of independent critical researchers in and out of government—many of them Jewish, by the way—indicates that the Zionist intriguers on Team B did indeed exaggerate Soviet imperial designs and military strategy as Paisley and other unbiased analysts contended.

TEAM B MOVES TO TAKE COMMAND

In the end, the behind-the-scenes Team B experiment inside the upper ranks of the US intelligence community laid the groundwork for the modern-day "neo-conservative" network that ultimately assumed control of the Bush administration beginning in 2001.

Writing in his scholarly (if vaguely-admiring) study of the neo-conservatives—*The Rise of Neoconservatism: Intellectuals and Foreign Affairs*—John Ehrman reports that the rejuvenation of the Cold War-era "blue ribbon" group known as the Committee on the Present Danger was a direct outgrowth of the Team B process, essentially a public relations approach to disseminating the Team B geopolitical outlook.[51]

Professor Benjamin Ginsberg notes in his history, *The Fatal Embrace: Jews & the State*, a study of the Jewish role in American political affairs, that veteran diplomat Paul Nitze of "Team B" fame and former Under Secretary of State Eugene Rostow were among the founders

of the new Committee, along with former Treasury Secretary Charls
Walker who was then serving as a lobbyist for defense contracting firms
that helped supply financing for the committee. The committee's general
counsel was Max Kampelman, a high-powered Washington figure known
as a key player in the Israeli lobby. Ginsberg candidly described the
nature of the organization:

> The Committee on the Present Danger, in effect, was an alliance between
> cold warriors . . . who believed in the need to contain the Soviet Union . . . the
> defense industry . . . which had an obvious pecuniary interest in heightened lev-
> els of defense spending, and pro-Israel forces who had come to see high levels
> of defense spending and an interventionist U.S. foreign policy as essential to
> Israel's survival and who hoped to make support for Israel an element of
> America's effort to contain the Soviet Union.
>
> Each of these allies had a stake in asserting that Soviet expansion represent-
> ed a "clear and present danger" to the United States. For cold warriors, this was
> political gospel as well as a route through which they hoped to return to power
> in the bureaucracy. For the defense industry, this was the key to high profits. For
> the Israel lobby, opposition to the USSR was a rubric through which to justify
> the expansion of American military and economic assistance to Israel.[52]
>
> Ginsberg pointed out that during the 1980 election campaign, the members
> of the committee became active in Ronald Reagan's presidential election effort
> and thus, the committee "became the vehicle through which the alliance of cold
> warriors, defense contractors, and pro-Israel groups became part of the Reagan
> coalition and gained access to the government."[53]

Ultimately, as noted by American historian, Richard Gid Powers,
Reagan brought no less than sixty members of the Committee into his
administration, including its founders, Paul Nitze and Eugene Rostow,
who were placed in the most critical arms control positions.[54]

The New York Times went so far as to assert that the Committee's
influence amounted to "a virtual takeover of the nation's national security apparatus."[55]

At the time the Reagan administration assumed office, many of the
same personalities involved in the activities of the Committee on the
Present Danger established yet another "blue ribbon" committee with
motivations parallel to the operations of the Committee on the Present
Danger.

Known as the Committee for a Free World, this new entity, founded by Midge Decter, wife of yet another ex-Trotskyite-turned-"neo-conser-vative," Norman Podhoretz, included among its members such individu-als as Elliott Abrams, Gertrude Himmelfarb (wife of Irving Kristol and mother of William Kristol) and Michael Ledeen, all of whom, today, are part of the "Perle-Kristol network." Notably, one of those who helped raise funds for this committee was Donald Rumsfeld, who is now prose-cuting the U.S. war against Iraq as Defense Secretary in the George W. Bush administration.[56]

The bottom line of all of this, as Team B critic Anne Hessing Cahn put it, is that "When Ronald Reagan got elected, Team B became, in essence, the A Team."[57] And the impact of Team B's false estimates is still affecting America into the beginning of the 21st century, not only in terms of foreign policy, but in domestic policy as well. Ms. Cahn notes:

> For more than a third of a century, perceptions about U.S. national security were colored by the view that the Soviet Union was on the road to military supe-riority over the United States. Neither Team B nor the multibillion dollar intelli-gence agencies could see that the Soviet Union was dissolving from within.
>
> For more than a third of a century, assertions of Soviet superiority created calls for the United States to "rearm." In the 1980s, the call was heeded so thor-oughly that the United States embarked on a trillion-dollar defense buildup.
>
> As a result, the country neglected its schools, cities, roads and bridges, and health care system. From the world's greatest creditor nation, the United States became the world's greatest debtor, in order to pay for arms to counter the threat of a nation that was collapsing.[58]

Certainly, there is no question that the institution of Team B and its resulting impact on US policy laid the groundwork for the future drive for power that brought the neo-conservatives (who had been groomed by Richard Perle through the Team B process) into outright control of poli-cy in the George W. Bush administration beginning in 2001.

And in those heady years of the Reagan era—and the rise of the Team B group—what turned out to be a pivotal event that would have immense future ramifications was the appointment of none other than Richard Perle as assistant secretary of defense for international security policy and Perle's subsequent recruitment as his own deputy his close friend and for-mer Capitol Hill crony, Stephen J. Bryen.

And therein lies a story in and of itself . . .

THE PERLE-BRYEN SPY SCANDAL

Although Perle and Bryen achieved immense power as high-level political appointees in the Reagan administration, their rise was nearly derailed by a scandal that erupted just two years prior to Reagan's election to the presidency. A complete understanding of this scandal is critical to understanding precisely how closely wed to the government of Israel that the Perle network truly is.

Let us begin by noting that in the era of the Team B intrigue (the mid-1970s)— Perle left Senator Jackson's staff and began engaging in the private arms business, setting up many lucrative deals between the Pentagon and Soltam, one of Israel's premier weapons firms.

Meanwhile, Perle's Capitol Hill associate, Stephen J. Bryen, was under observation by the FBI beginning as early as 1977 when he was suspected of using his post as a Senate Foreign Relations Committee staffer to obtain classified Pentagon information, particularly related to Arab military matters, that the Defense Intelligence Agency suspected Bryen was turning over to the Israelis.

Then, on March 9, 1978, Bryen was overheard in a private conversation over breakfast with four Israeli intelligence officials at the coffee shop of the Madison Hotel in Washington. It was clear, based on the content of his conversation, that he was providing the Israeli officials with high-level military information.

What was so amazing, however, was that Bryen (an American and a U.S. government employee) was heard continually referring to the U.S. government as "they" and to use the pronoun "we" when referring to his—and the Israeli government's—position. Little did Bryen know that an American of Arabic descent, who had been active in Arab-American affairs and lobbying on the Middle East issue, would recognize him (Bryen) and actually understand the sensitive nature of the conversation that Bryen was conducting with the Israeli officials.

The Arab-American businessman, one Michael Saba, reported the matter to the Federal Bureau of Investigation. In due course, a full-scale FBI inquiry into Bryen evolved to the point that the Justice Department (which oversees the FBI) assembled a 632-page file on Bryen's activities. The U.S. Attorney handling the investigation, Joel Lisker (an American of the Jewish faith) recommended that Bryen be indicted on felony charges of having not only been an unregistered foreign agent for Israel but also of having committed espionage on behalf of Israel.

The scandal finally broke (to a limited degree) in the American media, with the liberal journal, *The Nation*, making the allegation that Bryen had routinely taken orders from Zvi Rafiah, a counselor at the Israeli Embassy. In fact, it was ultimately learned, Rafiah was not just an embassy counselor. He was the U.S. station chief for the clandestine services division of Israel's intelligence agency, the Mossad.

Despite all this, Bryen was not indicted. Instead, Bryen was told to "quietly" depart from the Senate Foreign Relations Committee staff, which he did. Appropriately, Bryen promptly set up shop in Washington, D.C. as a publicist and lobbyist for Israel as the director of a group known as the Jewish Institute for National Security Affairs (JINSA).[59]

Ultimately, as we have seen, when Republican Ronald Reagan was elected president with firm support from the neo-conservative Jewish network, Perle and Bryen moved back into the upper ranks of the U.S. government policy making establishment—despite the scandal.

Perle was named Assistant Secretary of Defense for International Security Policy and quickly moved to bring in Bryen as his deputy for international economic trade and security policy. However, Perle became quite controversial for his own involvement with Israeli defense interests.

On April 17, 1983 *The New York Times* published a major story pointing out that there were ethics questions surrounding Perle's work for Zoltam, the major Israeli defense firm. Precisely at the time Perle entered the Defense Department he had accepted a $50,000 fee from Shlomo Zabludowitz, the founder of Zoltam, for work that he had done on behalf of the firm. Then, nearly a year later, while serving in the Defense Department, he urged the Secretary of the U.S. Army to consider doing business with Zabludowitz. Questions were raised as to whether this was a violation of U.S. laws governing the ethics of public officials, but Perle essentially escaped censure.

Ironically, similar ethics questions were raised about Perle's private business dealings in the days leading up to—and immediately after—the launch of the U.S. war against Iraq in March of 2003—some 20 years later. However, neither in 2003 (nor as previously) were serious questions raised about *the more inflammatory accusations* involving possible espionage by Perle and his friend and colleague Bryen on behalf of Israel.

In any event, Perle and Bryen became influential during the Reagan administration. In 1984, *Business Week* magazine noted of Perle: "To ensure that his views prevail, Perle has built up a powerful backstage network of allies in Washington."[60] By 1986 *The Washington Post* was quoting a senior U.S. State Department official as saying that Perle was "the most powerful man in the Pentagon"[61]—even more powerful than his actual superior, then-Secretary of Defense Caspar Weinberger.

This, however, did not prevent independent newspapers such as the aforementioned *Spotlight*, whose investigative journalist Andrew St. George pioneered coverage of the Bryen affair, from attempting to bring the matter to widespread public attention, assisted by the Arab-American businessman, Michael Saba, who had first seen and overheard Bryen's leak of classified information to the Israeli agents.

Nor did it prevent Saba and Arab-American organizations from continuing to lobby for a full-force inquiry into both the Bryen affair itself and the shadowy circumstances that led to the shelving of the Justice Department's intended prosecution of Bryen. Although Saba published a detailed book outlining the activities of Perle and Bryen, entitled *The Armageddon Network*, the Reagan administration (under pressure from the Israeli lobby) refused to "come clean" and investigate the Bryen affair

In fact, the stench surrounding the matter became so putrid that even a "mainstream" newspaper such as *The Boston Globe* was moved to assert editorially on Aug. 28, 1986: "Stopping espionage, maintaining a balance in relationships with Israel and its Arab neighbors, and avoiding even a hint of Israeli interference in formulation of US policy are all crucial to American interests in the Middle East. The Bryen case, which raised doubts on all counts, needs to be cleaned up." [62] In recent years, virtually the only major publication to even recall the Bryen affair is the Washington, DC-based *American Free Press*.

ISRAEL AND THE CHINA CARD

So it was that Perle and Bryen remained influential—and unbridled—during their years in the Defense Department under Republican Ronald Reagan. Yet, interestingly, during that period, despite their much perceived hard-line "anti-communism," Perle and Bryen emerged as perhaps the two chief promoters of Israel's lucrative (but largely little known) arms exports to communist China.

On Jan. 25, 1985, the very pro-Israel *Washington Times* reported that "Perle, the [Reagan] administration official most responsible for trying to deny US weapons technology to [Soviet-bloc] communist countries is said to favor the Israel-China arms link. Also said to favor the traffic is Stephen Bryen . . ."

To many American conservatives—traditional anti-communists—this was significant, particularly in light of Perle's reputation as an "anti-communist." However, on May 21, 1984, *Business Week* magazine reported that a congressional aide had said of Perle: "He's not a virulent anti-communist; he is a virulent anti-Soviet."

At the time, Perle's critics found significance in this comment, noting that, indeed, many of the "neo-conservatives" were, in fact, ostensibly "reformed" Trotskyites and that, perhaps, the "neo-conservative" war against the Soviet Union was hardly more than a continuation of an ideological battle that had begun between Josef Stalin and his chief rival, Leon Trotsky, and which continued to rage between their followers, even after Stalin and Trotsky were no longer alive.

It may not be a coincidence that former Republican Vice President Nelson Rockefeller once created a stir by actually calling Perle a "communist."[63] As cynics noted, although Rockefeller apologized, the outspoken and well-informed billionaire may have known something that most people did not.

JINSA—THE NEO-CONSERVATIVE WAR MACHINE

During the succeeding years, as Perle and Bryen continued to remain active in pro-Israel circles in Washington, their power and influence was heralded in *The Wall Street Journal* in an article entitled, "Roles of Ex-Pentagon Officials at Jewish Group Show Clout of Cold-Warrior, Pro-

Israel Network." The article described what the *Journal* called a "tight little circle [that] illustrated an enduring network of Cold War conservatives
and pro-Israel interests in Washington." Although the Cold War was over,
the *Journal* noted, "their political and governmental ties are a source of
influence for pro-Israeli forces."[64]

The article related the activities of the group known as the Jewish
Institute for National Security Affairs (or JINSA), which Perle's associ-
ate, Stephen Bryen, founded just prior to serving under Perle in the
Reagan administration. (During Bryen's government hiatus, JINSA was
run by Bryen's wife Shoshana). Describing JINSA's influence, the
Journal said:

> With little fanfare, JINSA itself has carved out a niche by both cultivating
> closer U.S.-Israeli military ties and urging U.S. Jews to vote for a strong defense
> at home. Building support in the Pentagon is a high priority. Under a program
> called "Send a General to Israel," hundreds of thousands of dollars in tax-
> deductible contributions bankroll an annual tour of Israel by retired U.S. gener-
> als and admirals. They exchange views with Israeli officials and tour strategic
> areas like the Golan Heights."[65]

Not by coincidence JINSA today (as noted earlier) is one of the prime
movers in the "neo-conservative" circles governing policy in the Bush
administration. Not only Vice President Dick Cheney, but Deputy Under
Secretary of Defense Douglas Feith were associated—as we have seen—
with JINSA prior to assuming office.

And this brings our discussion of the early years of the neo-conservative movement full circle, up to the events that occurred between Sept.
11, 2001 and the opening guns of the war against Iraq.

With his longtime friend Paul Wolfowitz working inside the Bush
administration, promoting all-out war against Israel's perceived enemies,
Perle joined William Kristol in assembling what amounts to a second-
generation version of "Team B" that is nothing less than a "War Party."

In the wake of the 9-11 attacks, Perle and Kristol hammered out a letter to the president echoing Wolfowitz' call for all-out war against Iraq,
Iran and Syria, not to mention the Palestinian Hezbollah. To supplement
their effort, they called upon a bevy of "neo-conservative" operatives—
along with a handful of "liberals"—to join them in signing the letter.

THE WAR PARTY—NAMING SOME NAMES

Although the list of signers is bipartisan and includes a number of persons identified with the "liberal" philosophy, the one thread of consistency is that, candidly, while most of persons on the list happen to be Jewish, those who are not have still been long-standing and enthusiastic members of what traditional American conservative Pat Buchanan, a critic of the neo-conservatives, called "Israel's Amen Corner" in official Washington.

All of the signers, likewise, have longstanding and intimate connections to the Kristol family network and their allies in the sphere of influence surrounding Richard Perle from the old "Team B" days of the 1970s. They are indeed the "war party." What follows is a virtual "who's who" of the imperial war party.

Gary Bauer. Another longtime satellite of Irving Kristol and his son William (with whom he shared an interest in a vacation condominium), Bauer has been a strong and unswerving advocate for Israel inside the American "Christian Right" movement through his leadership of the Family Research Council.

William J. Bennett. Bennett's entire career in official Washington has come with the patronage of the Kristol family, ranging from his post as chairman of the National Endowment for the Humanities and then as secretary of education under President Ronald Reagan and as "drug czar" under President George H. W. Bush. Bennett is a co-director of a Kristol-sponsored "think tank" known as Empower America, founded in 1991. In return for Irving Kristol's sponsorship, Bennett gave William Kristol his first high-level job in government, naming him chief of staff at the U.S. Department of Education.

Eliot Cohen. The director of the Center for Strategic Education at the [Paul] Nitze School of Advanced International Studies (SAIS)—of which former deputy secretary of defense Paul Wolfowitz served as dean, prior to his return to the Defense Department—Cohen is the author of a new book devoted to the subject of "Israel's security revolution."

Midge Decter. The wife of Council on Foreign Relations figure Norman Podhoretz [see below] and a widely-promoted media figure in her own right, Decter is the mother of John Podhoretz who has been a deputy editor of *The Weekly Standard*, of which William Kristol is editor and publisher.

Thomas Donnelly. The deputy director of William Kristol's Project for the New American Century, and a former executive editor of *The National Interest*, a "neo-conservative" journal founded by Kristol's father, Irving Kristol, Donnelly is a veteran military correspondent who was trained at the Johns Hopkins' University's SAIS, where (as noted previously) Paul Wolfowitz served as dean prior to returning to the Defense Department.

Hillel Fradkin. An outspoken Zionist who is a "resident fellow" at the American Enterprise Institute and an adjunct professor of government at Georgetown University, Fradkin is the Washington director of the Israeli-based Shalem Center which describes itself as a "research institute for Jewish and Israeli social thought." Fradkin has also served as a vice president of the Lynde and Harry Bradley Foundation, a "conservative" foundation which has provided millions of dollars in funding to myriad pro-Israel (and anti-Arab and anti-Islamic) groups and projects. Of course, it is no coincidence that, in earlier years, William Kristol had been associated with this foundation and continues to be a major player in directing its affairs.

Frank Gaffney. A major player in the Perle-Kristol sphere, Gaffney is the "hawkish" director of the Center for Security Policy—a Washington think tank known for what has been described as support for "extreme right-wing Israeli causes," and which includes Richard Perle on its board of advisors. Gaffney himself worked alongside Perle on the staff of Sen. Henry M. Jackson when Perle was active in establishing "Team B" and operating as an asset in place for Israel. Gaffney's board of directors also includes former American-Israel Public Affairs Committee director Morris Amitay, as well as former Navy Secretary John Lehman [see below]. Gaffney's CSP receives funding from the Irving I. Moskowitz Foundation which has supported real estate takeovers in Israel associated with Israeli Prime Minister Ariel Sharon and from the aforementioned Kristol-influenced Lynde and Harry Bradley Foundation. Gaffney specializes in training pro-Israel interns for insertion into public policy-making posts in government and providing pro-Israel-oriented propaganda for distribution in Republican and "conservative" circles. Gaffney is a widely-quoted columnist who writes for the "neo-conservative" *Washington Times* newspaper.

Reuel Marc Gerecht. A former Middle Eastern specialist in the CIA's directorate of operations ("black ops") division, Gerecht's writing is featured in Kristol-associated publications such as *The Weekly Standard*. He is protégé of Richard Perle.

Michael Joyce. Little known to the general public, Joyce, yet another protege of Irving Kristol, is a former school teacher who has risen to power through his involvement with a number of well-heeled foundations known for sponsoring pro-Israel causes, including the Olin Foundation—funded by chemical and munitions interests—which has sponsored anti-Islamic propaganda by writer Steven Emerson (a widely-cited "authority" on "Islamic terrorism" and the (again, aforementioned) Lynde and Harry Bradley Foundation, of which he (Joyce) was the longtime director. The Bradley Foundation has been a major font of funding for National Affairs, Inc., the Kristol family-associated enterprise that publishes *The National Interest* and *The Public Interest* magazines.

Donald Kagan. A widely-published historian with an interest in the history of warfare and an advocate—like William Kristol—of flexing American military power worldwide, Kagan is a professor of classics and history at Yale University.

Robert Kagan. The son of Donald Kagan, mentioned above, he is director of William Kristol's Project for the New American Century, a senior associate at the Carnegie Endowment for International Peace, and also a contributing editor of Kristol's *Weekly Standard* and writes a regular monthly column for the *Washington Post* where he consistently touts a staunch pro-Israel line and advocates U.S. meddling abroad. (Robert Kagan's brother, Frederick Kagan, has also emerged as a leading figure in the neo-conservative power network as well.)

Charles Krauthammer. A well-known television "talking head" and nationally-syndicated newspaper columnist, Krauthammer, who was trained as a psychiatrist, seems obsessed with devoting all of his waking hours writing and talking about the need for the United States to devote its energies to the preservation of Israel and the destruction of Israel's enemies. His venom for critics of Israel is perhaps unmatched.

John Lehman. A former National Security Council (NSC) advisor to

then-Secretary of State Henry Kissinger, Lehman went on to serve as
Navy Secretary during the Reagan administration and as deputy director
of the U.S. Arms Control and Disarmament Agency where he was closely associated with the intimate pro-Israel circles surrounding Paul
Wolfowitz and Richard Perle. British journalist Claudia Wright notes that
before he became Navy Secretary Lehman "was well-known in Israeli
military circles, sat on the board of a Philadelphia think tank run by
American supporters of Israel, and operated a highly profitable defense
consulting company with business ties to the Israeli arms industry." Along
with Perle, and other Kristol family cronies previously mentioned,
Lehman is a member of the board of advisors of the Center for Security
Policy [See Frank Gaffney, above].

Martin Peretz. The stridently pro-Israel publisher of the "liberal"
New Republic, Peretz declared in the Sept. 24 edition of his magazine
that, in the wake of the terrorist attacks on 9-11 that "we are all Israelis
now." Very much an ally of the neo-conservatives, Peretz has long been
recognized as a key figure in a network of top-level publishers and media
figures allied with one goal in mind: promoting the cause of Israel.

Norman Podhoretz. A Council on Foreign Relations member and a
key figure in the influential New York chapter of the American Jewish
Committee and its "liberal-turned-conservative" *Commentary* magazine,
Podhoretz is another "ex-Trotskyite" who emerged as one of the leaders
of the pro-Israel neo-conservative crowd in association with Irving
Kristol. His son, John Podhoretz, was a colleague of William Kristol as
deputy editor of the Rupert Murdoch-financed *Weekly Standard*.

Stephen J. Solarz. A former longtime member of the House of
Representatives where he was a major legislative legman for the interests
of Israel, Solarz is now a high-powered international consultant. While in
Congress, Solarz played a major role (in league with Paul Wolfowitz, then
serving in the Reagan administration) in the overthrow of former
Philippine President Ferdinand Marcos when the Asian leader attempted
to assert his nation's sovereignty.

Vin Weber. A former member of the House of Representatives where
he was an energetic (non-Jewish) supporter of Israel, Weber was a co-
founder of William Kristol's Empower America and in the 2000 presidential campaign was a top advisor to Sen. John McCain (R-Ariz.). While

in the House, Weber helped sabotage an effort to force a congressional investigation of Israel's terroristic 1967 attack on the *U.S.S. Liberty* which resulted in the murder of 34 American sailors and the maiming of 172 others. Weber is also a member of the Council on Foreign Relations.

Marshall Wittmann. Although he is Jewish, Wittman was the director of legislative affairs for the pro-Israel Christian Coalition. Wittmann's advocacy of "National Greatness Conservatism"—that is U.S. meddling overseas and the flexing of U.S. military might on Israel's behalf—has been promoted in the pages of William Kristol's *Weekly Standard*.

While this is a representative overview of many of the people in the Perle-Kristol network, it is by no means complete. But it does illustrate the amazing power and influence that Kristol and his associates—The High Priests of War—have assembled.

Kristol's magazine, *The Weekly Standard*, is the officially recognized media voice for this combine, to the point that although its actual circulation is quite small Kristol's magazine is generally recognized by most other major media as certainly one of the most influential publications in America—bar none.

KRISTOL'S WAR?

It was not so extraordinary then, that, on March 17, 2003—the day before the United States launched the war against Iraq, Kristol was able to brag in a signed editorial in *The Weekly Standard* that "obviously, we are gratified that the Iraq strategy we have long advocated . . . has become the policy of the U.S. government."[66]

Just one day later, on March 18, as the war began, *The Washington Post* reminded its readers how influential Kristol was, noting that the *Post*'s columnist, Richard Cohen, had once declared the looming conflict to be "Kristol's War." *The Post* wrote of Kristol that with U.S. forces on the verge of bombing Baghdad, "this would seem to be Kristol's moment."[67]

For the beleaguered people of Iraq and for the American and British soldiers who died in pursuit of the neo-conservative war aims—and for the American taxpayers, who must pay the bills—it was not their moment, however much Kristol and company may have rejoiced.

ABANDONING TRADITIONAL AMERICAN POLICY

We have seen how this new form of "conservative imperialism" with roots in the ranks of an elite group of "former" Trotskyite leftists—who have transformed into Republican "neo-conservatives"—has taken hold of the reins of power at the highest ranks of the administration of President George W. Bush. This conservative imperialism is the foundation upon which the current war against Iraq is based and upon which future imperial American wars in the Middle East and elsewhere are likewise hinged.

It is these neo-conservatives who support a modern-day brand of imperialism—the concept of U.S. interventionism and meddling abroad. The ongoing war against Iraq is the culmination of a long-standing drive by the neo-conservatives who view the war as the first step in a long-ranging plan to not only "remake the Arab world," but also to establish the United States as the sole world power, unquestioned in military and economic might.

This political philosophy—"neo-conservatism"—has virtually rewritten, even supplanted, the traditional "conservative" point of view exemplified by Republican nationalists such as the late Sen. Robert A. Taft, a leading figure in American political affairs during the mid-20th century. Taft and others who shared his views did not believe it was the duty of America to play "world policeman." Taft and his like-minded colleagues believed that America's first duty was to attend to the needs of its own people and not meddle in the affairs of other nations.

The very "liberal" Democratic Party-oriented *Washington Post*—perhaps America's most powerful daily newspaper—was never fond of the conservative "America First" viewpoint of Taft and his political heirs.

However, in the past decade, as the so-called "neo-conservative" element began to infiltrate and, ultimately, take control of the American conservative movement and the upper ranks of the Republican Party, increasingly advocating an aggressive internationalist worldview, the *Post* began to trumpet the so-called "neo-conservatives."

On Aug. 21, 2001 the *Post* featured an article entitled, "Empire or Not? A quiet debate over U.S. role" which it billed as one in a series of occasional articles focusing on "Ideas from the Right." The article—which was evidently a good publicity boost for the "neo-cons"— opened by commenting:

> People who label the United States "imperialist" usually mean it as an insult. But in recent years a handful of conservative defense intellectuals have begun to argue that the United States is indeed acting in an imperialist fashion—and that it should embrace the role.[68]

The *Post* said that this is idea of enforcing a new "Pax Americana" was part of a "vigorous, expansionistic Reaganite foreign policy" that makes the United States, in the *Post*'s words, "an empire of democracy or liberty." Under this new form of imperialism, the United States is not conquering land or establishing colonies in the style of the old British and Roman empires, but instead "has a dominating global presence military, economically and culturally."[69]

The *Post* noted, as an example, that one of the foremost advocates of this new imperialism was Thomas Donnelly, deputy executive director of the Project for the New American Century, the Washington think tank founded by William Kristol.

THE FIRST IMPERIAL OFFENSIVE FAILED

Ironically, during the earlier administration of George H. W. Bush—father of the current American president—the hard-line neo-conservative forces tried, but failed, to enunciate the very policies of imperial power now being pursued by the younger Bush.

After the first President Bush decided to withdraw from Iraq during the first war in the Arabian Gulf, then-Secretary of Defense Dick Cheney (now vice president) circulated the draft of a document, prepared under the direction of neo-conservative Paul Wolfowitz, which advocated American global unilateralism, abandoning traditional American alliances.

Notably, the proposal suggested the United States should consider pre-emptive force of the very type ultimately used against Iraq in 2003. However, when the document was leaked to the press, the senior President Bush, in the words of American author Michael Lind, "quickly distanced [himself and his administration] from the radicalism of the Cheney-Wolfowitz report."[70]

That Cheney should have been so enamored with the neo-conservative position surprised no one. For some years Cheney had been associated with the Richard Perle-connected lobby for Israel known as the Jewish Institute for National Security Affairs (JINSA), founded by Perle's long-time friend Stephen Bryen who had been investigated for espionage on behalf of Israel. (That JINSA link is ubiquitous. It *won't* go away!)

It was not until the advent of the second Bush administration—under George W. Bush—that the neo-conservatives finally won the day and their drive for an imperial policy, centered on the proposed assault on Iraq, finally achieved success.

In fact, by the time that the American war against Iraq finally erupted in March of 2003, the "quiet" debate over imperialism described by the *Washington Post* was no longer quiet.

Leading the side of the debate favoring American imperialism was William Kristol, along with allies inside the Bush administration such as Paul Wolfowitz, now the number two man in the Defense Department, his deputy, Douglas Feith, and others, all of whom were actively supported by Richard Perle, by this point ensconced as chairman of the Bush administration's Defense Policy Board.

So it was that once the long-promoted war against Iraq was already under way the concept of "American Empire" was very much the subject of public discussion in the American elite media and in many intellectual journals. As Jeet Heer pointed out in *The Boston Globe* on March 23, 2003, just days after the first American assault on Iraq:

> Since the Sept. 11 attacks . . . many foreign policy pundits, mostly from the Republican right but also including some liberal internationalists, have revisited the idea of empire.
>
> "America is the most magnanimous imperial power ever," declared Dinesh D'Souza in *The Christian Science Monitor* in 2002. "Afghanistan and other troubled lands today cry out for the sort of enlightened foreign administration once provided by self-confident Englishmen in jodhpurs and pith helmets," argued Max Boot in a 2001 article for *The Weekly Standard* titled "The Case for American Empire."
>
> In *The Wall Street Journal*, historian Paul Johnson asserted that the "answer to terrorism" is "colonialism." Columnist Mark Steyn, writing in *The Chicago Sun-Times*, has contended that "imperialism is the answer."
>
> "People are now coming out of the closet on the word 'empire'," noted *Washington Post* columnist Charles Krauthammer. "The fact is no country has been as dominant culturally, economically, technologically and militarily in the history of world since the Roman Empire."[71]

In fact, of all of the above-mentioned writers—D'Souza, Boot, Johnson, Steyn and Krauthammer—are among the energetic clique of media analysts promoting the neo-conservative worldview.

U.S. OPPOSITION TO NEO-CONSERVATIVE IMPERIALISM

However, there does remain opposition to the imperial philosophy of the "neo-conservative" network.

Perhaps the foremost nationally-known critic of the neo-conservatives is columnist Pat Buchanan who raised the banner of American nationalism (as opposed to internationalism and imperialism) in his presidential campaign on the Reform Party ticket in 2000. Buchanan, a lifelong Republican, went to the Reform Party after realizing that his effort to restore traditional nationalism to the Republican Party was going nowhere. Buchanan's book, *A Republic, Not an Empire*, was a clarion call for grass-roots opposition to the drive for a "Pax Americana."

As such, after the drive for war against Iraq took hold in official policy making circles in the Bush administration, Buchanan offered the pages of his newly-established *American Conservative* magazine to enunciate the dangers in the new imperialism being propounded by the "neo-conservative" network.

One particular exposition appearing in Buchanan's magazine, written by Andrew Bacevich, a retired American army colonel who is a professor of international relations at Boston University, is probably among the best and most succinct specific analyses of what the new American imperialism constitutes:

> All but lost amidst the heated talk of regime change in Baghdad, the White House in late September [2002] issued the Bush administration's *U.S. National Security Strategy*.
>
> The Bush USNSS offers the most comprehensive statement to date of America's globe-straddling post-Cold War ambitions. In it, the administration makes plain both its intention to perpetuate American military supremacy and its willingness—almost approaching eagerness—to use force to reshape the international order.
>
> This new strategy places the approaching showdown with Saddam Hussein in a far wider context, showing that overthrowing the Iraqi dictator is only the next step in a massive project, pursued under the guise of the "war on terror," but aimed ultimately at remaking the world in our image.

Hence, the second major theme of the new U.S. National Security Strategy—a candid acknowledgment and endorsement of the progressively greater militarization of U.S. foreign policy.

To state the point bluntly, the Bush administration no longer views force as the last resort; rather, it considers military power to be America's most effective instrument of statecraft—the area in which the United States owns the greatest advantage.

Beginning with the premise that "our best defense is a good offense," the USNSS describes how President Bush intends to exploit that advantage to the fullest.

He will do so in two ways. First, he will expand U.S. global power projection capabilities. Already spending roughly as much on defense as the entire rest of the world combined, the United States will spend still more—much, much more.

The purpose of this increase is not to respond to any proximate threat. Rather, the Bush administration is boosting the Pentagon's budget with an eye toward achieving a margin of such unprecedented and unsurpassed superiority that no would-be adversary will even consider mounting a future challenge. The United States will thereby secure in perpetuity its status as sole superpower. Old concerns about the "clashing wills of powerful states" will disappear; henceforth, a single power will call the tune.

Second, with the USNSS codifying the concept of "anticipatory self-defense," President Bush claims for the United States the prerogative of using force preemptively and unilaterally, however its interests may dictate. (That prerogative belongs exclusively to the United States: the Bush strategy pointedly warns other nations not to "use preemption as a pretext for aggression.") In contrast to his predecessor's reactive, half-hearted military adventures, Bush will employ America's armed might proactively and on a scale sufficient to achieve rapid, decisive results. The prospect of ever greater U.S. military activism—against terrorists, against rogue states, against evildoers of whatever stripe—beckons.

Nowhere does the Bush administration's national security strategy pause to consider whether the nation's means are adequate to the "great mission" to which destiny has ostensibly summoned the United States. Asserting that American global hegemony is necessarily benign and that Washington can be counted on to use the Bush Doctrine of preemption judiciously, nowhere does it contemplate the possibility that others might take a contrary view.

In truth, whatever their party affiliation or ideological disposition, members of the so-called foreign policy elite cannot conceive of an alternative to "global leadership"—the preferred euphemism for global empire.[72]

Although coming from a traditional "conservative"—as opposed to the "neo-conservative" viewpoint—Bacevich does not stand alone in these concerns. In fact, even liberal American writers have expressed similar fears of the new drive for an American empire.

Writing in the progressive journal, *Mother Jones*, author Todd Gitlin echoed much of what Bacevich expressed. Gitlin referred likewise to the new Bush administration policy document and declared:

> The document is meant not so much to be read as to be brandished. This is internationalism imperial-style—as in Rome, when Rome ruled. Its scope is breath-taking. There were large parts of the world that Rome couldn't reach, but the Bush doctrine recognizes no limits.
>
> It will know when threats are emerging, partly formed, and it will not have to say how it knows, or be convincing about what it knows. The doctrine affirms all of the comforts and recognizes none of the dangers of empire.
>
> It ignores the costs of unbounded deployment and war. It acknowledges no danger that reckless swashbuckling helps recruit terrorists. It forgets that all empires fall—they cost too much, incite too many enemies, they inspire contrary empires. The new imperialists think they are different. All empires do.[73]

Gitlin concluded (correctly) that the American government is "hell-bent on empire and has said so in black and white."[74]

AMERICAN ZIONIST SUPPORT FOR IMPERIALISM

Despite these criticisms, very powerful interests in the American political arena were very much pleased by the new imperialism being pursued by the Bush administration. Exemplifying this support was a notable essay by Norman Podhoretz appearing in the Sept. 2002 issue of *Commentary* magazine, the influential neo-conservative journal published by the influential New York chapter of the American Jewish Committee, one of the leading Zionist organizations on American soil.

Podhoretz, as we have seen, was one of the "founding fathers" in the establishment of the neo-conservative network that ultimately assumed supreme power in the ruling councils inside the Bush administration. An early protégé of William Kristol's father, Irving Kristol, "godfather" of the neo-conservatives, Podhoretz remains today a highly regarded senior figure in the neo-conservative movement.

As such, Podhoretz' assessment of the new policies is of special interest, particularly since Podhoretz freely acknowledges that the ultimate aim of the Bush policy, if carried to its utmost, would be the subjugation of the Arab Middle East as we know it today.

In his essay, Podhoretz asserted, in a somewhat mystical fashion, that following the Sept. 11 terrorist tragedy that rocked America, "a kind of revelation, blazing with a very different fire of its own, lit up the recesses of Bush's mind and heart and soul.

"Which is to say," added Podhoretz, "that having previously been unsure as to why he should have been chosen to become President of the United States, George W. Bush now *knew* that the God to whom, as a born-again Christian, he had earlier committed himself had put him in the Oval Office for a purpose. He had put him there to lead a war against the evil of terrorism."[75]

Thus, Podhoretz seemed to suggest that Bush was driven toward his course of imperialism and war against the Arab world by his Christian fundamentalist point of view. (And Podhoretz is probably right!)

Podhoretz then commented that Bush's first major address on Sept. 20, following the terrorist attacks, "may well have been the greatest presidential speech of our age," adding pointedly that Bush was actually abandoning even his own father's point of view.

"It was here," said Podhoretz, "that Bush's conversion from a conventional 'realist' in the mold of his father to a democratic 'idealist' of the Reaganite stamp was announced to the world."[76]

Declaring his support for the new Bush agenda, Podhoretz hailed the ultimate consequences of this policy as Podhoretz and his fellow neo-conservatives see it:

> The regimes that richly deserve to be overthrown and replaced are not confined to the three singled-out members of the axis of evil [that is, Iraq, Iran and North Korea].
>
> At a minimum, the axis should extend to Syria and Lebanon and Libya, as well as "friends" of America like the Saudi royal family and Egypt's Hosni Mubarak, along with the Palestinian Authority, whether headed by Arafat or one of his henchmen.
>
> There is no denying that the alternative to these regimes could easily turn out to be worse, even (or especially) if it comes into power through democratic elections. After all, by every measure we possess, very large numbers of people in the Muslim world sympathize with Osama bin Laden and would vote for radical Islamic candidates of his stripe if they were given the chance.

To dismiss this possibility would be the height of naiveté. Nevertheless, there is a policy that can head it off, provided that the United States has the will to fight World War IV—the war against militant Islam—to a successful conclusion, and provided, too, that we then have the stomach to impose a new political culture on the defeated parties.

This is what we did directly and unapologetically in Germany and Japan after winning World War II . . . There was a song that became popular in America during World War II: "We did it before, and we can do it again." What I am trying to say to the skeptics and the defeatists of today is that yes indeed we did it before; and yes indeed we can do it again.[77]

That these are aggressive and war-like words and presumptions is obvious. But the fact is that these words represent a point of view that has reached supreme influence at the highest levels of the administration that governs the most powerful nation on the face of the planet.

THE MILITARY CLASHES WITH THE NEO-CONSERVATIVES

However, the American military leadership did not agree with the neo-conservatives that an invasion of Iraq would either result in a mass uprising by the Iraqi people against Saddam (in alliance with U.S. forces) or that the rest of the Arab world would sit back with satisfaction. Nor did the American military even want to fight the war in the first place. The military leaders saw no need for the United States to enter into conflict with Iraq, viewing such a war as contrary to American national interests.

The idea that the American military leadership somehow favored the war with Iraq was a myth that was widely being propagated by the neo-conservative pro-Israel propaganda network in official Washington with the active support of the pro-Israel elements in the American media.

Following the terrorist attacks of Sept. 11, 2001, major media headlines and talking-heads on the broadcast networks in the United States repeatedly and relentlessly reported that "the Pentagon" was gearing up for a U.S.-led invasion of Iraq—this despite the fact there was no genuine evidence of any Iraqi instigation or involvement in the attacks whatsoever. (And no such evidence has emerged to this day.)

In any event, in the average American's perception, the idea that the war was being promoted by "the Pentagon" conjured up popular images of much-admired, heroic, battle-tested medal-laden generals and admirals chomping at the bit to "get Saddam."

There was just one big problem with the reports in the American media. The truth was that the career military men inside the Pentagon didn't think an invasion of Iraq was feasible or necessary. They saw it as a potential disaster for the United States that could ultimately align the United States (standing alone with Israel) against the entire Arab and Muslim world. In fact, precisely because of the military's opposition to the war against Iraq, the neo-conservative pro-Israel network at the highest levels of the Bush administration began laying the insidious groundwork to oust American military leaders who opposed U.S. involvement in a war against Iraq. That little-noticed fact was buried in a lengthy report published in *The Washington Post* on August 1, 2002. According to *Post* writer Thomas E. Ricks:

> At a July 10 meeting of the Defense Policy Board, a Pentagon advisory group, one of the subjects discussed was how to overcome the military reluctance to plan innovatively for an attack on Iraq.
> "What was discussed was the problem with the services," said one defense expert who participated in the meeting. His conclusion: "You have to have a few heads roll, especially in the Army."[78]

It is no coincidence that the Defense Policy Board (DPB) would be the point of origin of a plan to make "heads roll" inside the military. Although ostensibly "independent," the DPB was dominated at the time (and basically remains so) by Richard Perle who—although he never served in the U.S. military—made a fortune in armaments profiteering on behalf of Israel's military-industrial complex and has spent years promoting U.S. military engagements to defend the interests of Israel.

Regarding the ongoing conflict between the civilian pro-Israel neo-conservatives and the military leadership, the *Post* stated flatly on July 28, 2002 that:

> Despite President Bush's repeated bellicose statements about Iraq, many senior U.S. military officials contend that President Saddam Hussein poses no immediate threat and that the United States should continue its policy of containment rather than invade Iraq to force a change of leadership in Baghdad.
> The military's support of containment, and its concern about the possible negative consequences of attacking Iraq, are shared by senior officials at the State Department and the CIA, according to people familiar with interagency discussions.[79]

However, the *Post* pointed out: "High level civilians in the White House and Pentagon vehemently disagree." Those un-named "high-level" civilians were the neo-conservative warhawks such as Perle and his long-time associate and closest ally inside the Bush administration, Deputy Secretary of Defense Paul Wolfowitz and his lieutenant, Douglas Feith.

The Washington Post also reported that while "active duty members of the military have not publicly questioned the direction of Bush's Iraq policy [in] private some are very doubtful about it." The *Post* added:

> Retired officers and experts who stay in touch with the top brass, and are free to say what those on active duty cannot, are more outspoken in supporting the containment policy and questioning the administration's apparent determination to abandon it.[80]

Secretary of State Colin Powell—who served two tours of combat duty in Vietnam—was, in fact, initially aligned with the military brass in opposition to the Iraq war. Quite notably, General Tommy Franks—who ultimately led the American war against Iraq—also opposed the war.

Even the June 2002 issue of *The Washington Monthly*—an eminently "mainstream" liberal journal—featured a cover story about the "get Iraq" group and acknowledged frankly who they are: most of those in question, the magazine admitted, are "Jewish, passionately pro-Israel, and pro-Likud."[81] The magazine noted that the neo-conservative "hawks" are "united by a shared idea: that America should be unafraid to use its military power early and often to advance its interests and values."[82]

However, as *Washington Monthly* affirmed, this sabre-rattling philosophy "is an idea that infuriates most members of the national security establishment at the Pentagon, State, and the CIA, who believe that America's military force should be used rarely and only as a last resort, preferably in concert with allies."[83]

Yet, this war-driven and aggressive minority of sabre-rattlers has risen to supreme heights of power within official Washington and they are now making their influence felt.

In fact, as the drive for war intensified, the pro-Israel "palace guard" led by Paul Wolfowitz and surrounding Defense Secretary Donald Rumsfeld was trying to re-make the Pentagon, moving against America's top military officials who objected to fighting unnecessary imperial wars around the globe that have nothing to do with defending America.

Although many grassroots Americans believed that the Bush administration and Defense Secretary Donald Rumsfeld were strongly supported by America's military leadership, the truth was quite the opposite. While Bush came into office with quite enthusiastic support from American military families, the truth is that the active duty military leaders in the Pentagon were very much dissatisfied with Rumsfeld and his neo-conservative associates such as Wolfowitz.

An eye-opening profile of Rumsfeld, published in *The Washington Post* on Oct. 16, 2002 laid bare at least some of the little-known details surrounding the efforts by Rumsfeld and his pro-Israel "palace guard" to grab control of the Pentagon. Describing the Pentagon as "thick with tension," the *Post* stated flat out that:

> Many senior officers on the Joint Staff and in all branches of the military describe Rumsfeld as frequently abusive and indecisive, trusting only a tiny circle of close advisers, seemingly eager to slap down officers with decades of distinguished service.
>
> The unhappiness is so pervasive that all three service secretaries [Army, Navy and Air Force] are said to be deeply frustrated by a lack of autonomy and contemplating leaving by the end of the year.
>
> All three find their actions constrained by Rumsfeld and what is referred to as his small "palace guard," according to Pentagon insiders.[84]

While the *Post* named no names, the identity of the "palace guard" is no mystery. One defense consultant told the *Post* that "The depth of disaffection is really quite striking," adding that, in his view, "Rumsfeld is courting a rebellion." The *Post* asserted that Rumsfeld and his associates had the military's governing Joint Chiefs of Staff and its 1,200-member staff "in the cross hairs."[85]

Rumsfeld and Wolfowitz were trying to limit the ability of America's top military leaders from reaching out to Congress, government agencies and the media, by stripping the Joint Staff of its legislative liaison, legal counsel and public affairs offices, which, in the past, according to the *Post,* "have given the military leadership a degree of autonomy by providing it direct pipelines to Congress, to other parts of the government and to the media."[86]

In fact, what Rumsfeld's neo-conservative clique was trying to do was to isolate the American military leadership from the American public, knowing that if more of the public knew that the military opposed war against Iraq, the public—likewise—would most likely share that view, conventionally trusting in the military's judgment.

In the end, as we now know, the "neo-conservatives" prevailed and the military's warnings were shut out and sidelined, much to the military's disgust. *Events in Iraq have since confirmed the military's fears.*

AMERICA'S LIKUD: THE NEO-CONSERVATIVES

What remains the guiding force behind the "neo-conservative" philosophy that sponsors this dream of American imperialism is perhaps the most "controversial" topic in America today—the role of hard-line Israeli Likud-style Zionism in shaping the policies of the "neo-conservatives" who direct policy in the Bush administration.

To recognize that the neo-conservative policy makers operating the engine of power in Washington are indeed largely Jewish and, in addition, wedded to "right wing" Zionism, is crucial to understanding the course of world affairs today.

Author Michael Lind, a harsh critic of neo-conservative principles, sums up the "three pillars" of the globalist doctrine being pursued: "American unilateralism, pre-emptive war, and the alignment of American foreign policy with that of Israel's right-wing leader Ariel Sharon. Each of these elements of George W. Bush's grand strategy represented a dramatic break with previous American foreign policy."[87]

Notably, one American Jewish writer summed up the Zionist dreams guiding the Bush policy, particularly vis-à-vis Iraq, for *Time* magazine, a publication that is controlled by Jewish financial interests revolving around the powerful family of Edgar Bronfman, longtime head of the World Jewish Congress. In an essay entitled "How Israel is Wrapped Up in Iraq," *Time* columnist Joe Klein wrote with candor:

> A stronger Israel is very much embedded in the rationale for war with Iraq. It is a part of the argument that dare not speak its name, a fantasy quietly cherished by the neo-conservative faction in the Bush Administration and by many leaders of the American Jewish community.

The fantasy involves a domino theory. The destruction of Saddam's Iraq will not only remove an enemy of long-standing but will also change the basic power equation in the region. It will send a message to Syria and Iran about the perils of support for Islamic terrorists.

It will send a message to the Palestinians too: Democratize and make peace on Israeli terms, or forget about a state of your own. In the wackiest scenario, it will lead to the collapse of the wobbly Hashemite monarchy in Jordan and the establishment of a Palestinian state on that nation's East Bank.

No one in the government ever actually says these things publicly (although some American Jewish leaders do). Usually, the dream is expressed in the mildest possible terms: "I have high hopes that the removal of Saddam will strengthen our democratic allies in the region," Senator Joe Lieberman told me last week.[88]

That the war against Iraq, and the overall policy guiding it, is founded in the philosophy of the hard-right Likud elements in Israel and their neo-conservative allies in America at the levers of power in the Bush administration is now becoming an open topic of discussion.

At the same time, the neo-conservative warmongers began driving a wedge between the United States and its European allies.

NEO-CONSERVATIVES ASSAULT EUROPEAN CRITICS

The leading voices of the pro-Israel "neo-conservative" movement in the United States began waging (and continue to wage) a relentless and unabashed campaign promoting "anti-Europeanism" among Americans. Few Americans, however, probably understood the geopolitical forces behind this campaign.

This "anti-Europeanism" came at precisely the time when European governments and massive numbers of European citizens were loudly rejecting the demand by the U.S.-Israel-Britain axis for war against Iraq and raising questions about Israel's brutal policies toward the Palestinians. This caused great dismay for the neo-conservatives.

The anti-European campaign by the neo-conservatives reached such a fever pitch that even the February 13, 2003 issue of *The New York Review of Books*, a leading "liberal" organ known for its sympathies for Israel, published a detailed article outlining the neo-conservative attack on Israel's European critics.

In an article entitled "Anti-Europeanism in America," author Timothy Garton Ash assembled a growing list of neo-conservative writers who have aimed their guns at Europe. Leading the list was Richard Perle who claimed that Europe has lost its "moral compass."

In case anyone might fail to understand the reason why the neo-conservatives have this newfound antipathy toward Europe, Ash's article explained the bottom line: that "The Middle East is both a source and a catalyst of what threatens to become a downward spiral of burgeoning European anti-Americanism and nascent American anti-Europeanism, each reinforcing the other."[89]

In other words, quite simply: Israel and its powerful American lobby are at the center—really, the cause—of the conflict, although Ash doesn't quite put it that way. Ash wrote:

> Anti-Semitism in Europe and its alleged connection to European criticism of the Sharon government, has been the subject of the most acid anti-European commentaries from conservative American columnists and politicians.
>
> Some of these critics are themselves not just strongly pro-Israel but also "natural Likudites," one liberal Jewish commentator explained . . .
>
> In a recent article Stanley Hoffman writes that they seem to believe in an "identity of interests between the Jewish state and the United States."[90]

Almost as if on cue, one of Richard Perle's and William Kristol's collaborators in the new "anti-Europeanist" drive, Robert Kagan, vocally joined the harsh chorus to promote anti-Europeanism to the reading audience of *The Washington Post*, the influential daily published in the nation's capital. Kagan's Jan. 31, 2003 opinion column was a veritable textbook of the neo-conservative "Hate Europe" crusade. Kagan wrote:

> In London . . . one finds Britain's finest minds propounding, in sophisticated language and melodious Oxford accents, the conspiracy theories . . . concerning the "neo-conservative" (read: Jewish) hijacking of American foreign policy . . . In Paris, all the talk is of oil and "imperialism" (and Jews). In Madrid, it's oil, imperialism, past American support for Franco (and Jews).
>
> At a conference I recently attended in Barcelona, an esteemed Spanish intellectual asked why, if the United States wants to topple vicious dictatorships that manufacture weapons of mass destruction, it is not also invading Israel.
>
> Yes, I know, there are Americans who ask such questions, too . . . But here's

what Americans need to understand: In Europe, this paranoid, conspiratorial anti-Americanism is not a far-left or far-right phenomenon. It's the mainstream view.[91]

So it was that America's traditional European allies had now allied against the United States and the neo-conservative policy dictators who were spearheading a drive for a new imperialism. It was a formula that many American critics of the neo-conservatives believed would ultimately spell disaster, for not only America but the world.

THE ALLIANCE BETWEEN BUSH AND SHARON

So although traditional American policy has been thrown out the door—to the dismay of many articulate critics of the neo-conservative philosophy—there is yet another factor regarding the foundation of the neo-conservative point of view that must be considered: the resulting impact on the specific aspect of the U.S. "special relationship" with Israel.

Although American governments—ruled by both Democrats and Republicans alike—have always been heavily partial to Israel, no secret to anyone, the fact is that the ascendance of the neo-conservatives in the Bush administration has led to a virtual merger of U.S. foreign policy with the point of view of the hard-line "right wing" Likud bloc of Ariel Sharon and Israel.

Writing in *The Washington Post* on February 9, 2003, Robert G. Kaiser laid out the parameters of the Bush administration's unswerving alliance with the "right wing" of Israel. Kaiser's article, titled "Bush and Sharon Nearly Identical on Mideast Policy," was a forthright assertion of the power of the "neo-conservatives" in directing the administration's approach to Israel and the Arab world. The article said, in part:

> For the first time, a U.S. administration and a Likud government in Israel are pursuing nearly identical policies. Earlier U.S. administrations, from Jimmy Carter's through Bill Clinton's, held Likud and Sharon at arm's length, distancing the United States from Likud's traditionally tough approach to the Palestinians. But today . . . Israel and the United States share a common view on terrorism, peace with the Palestinians, war with Iraq and more.

The Bush administration's alignment with Sharon delights many of its strongest supporters, especially evangelical Christians, and a large part of organized American Jewry, according to leaders in both groups, who argue that Palestinian terrorism pushed Bush to his new stance.

"The Likudniks are really in charge now," said a senior government official, using a Yiddish term for supporters of Sharon's political party.

Some Middle East hands who disagree with these supporters of Israel refer to them as "a cabal," in the words of one former official. Members of the group do not hide their friendships and connections, or their loyalty to strong positions in support of Israel and Likud.

Richard Perle, chairman of the Pentagon's Defense Policy Board, led a study group that proposed to Binyamin Netanyahu, a Likud prime minister of Israel from 1996 to 1999, that he abandon the Oslo peace accords negotiated in 1993 and reject the basis for them — the idea of trading "land for peace." Israel should insist on Arab recognition of its claim to the biblical land of Israel, the 1996 report suggested, and should "focus on removing Saddam Hussein from power in Iraq."

Besides Perle, the study group included David Wurmser, now a special assistant to Undersecretary of State John R. Bolton, and Douglas J. Feith, now undersecretary of defense for policy. Feith has written prolifically on Israeli-Arab issues for years, arguing that Israel has as legitimate a claim to the West Bank territories seized after the Six Day War as it has to the land that was part of the U.N.-mandated Israel created in 1948.

An internal debate split the administration and invited the lobbying of think tanks, Jewish organizations, evangelical Christians and others who take a fierce interest in the Middle East . . .

Over the past dozen years or more, supporters of Sharon's Likud Party have moved into leadership roles in most of the American Jewish organizations that provide financial and political support for Israel.[92]

Writing shortly thereafter in *The Washington Times*—the neo-conservative oriented daily "rival" to the more "liberal" *Washington Post*—well-known journalist Arnaud deBorchgrave echoed Kaiser and elaborated on the topic of the new alliance between the Bush and Sharon regimes. In an article entitled "A Bush-Sharon Doctrine," deBorchgrave wrote, in part:

The strategic objectives of the U.S. and Israel in the Middle East have gradually merged into a now cohesive Bush-Sharon Doctrine. But this gets lost in the deafening cacophony of talking heads playing armchair generals in the coming war to change regimes in Baghdad.

Mr. Sharon provided the geopolitical ammo by convincing Mr. Bush that the war on Palestinian terrorism was identical to the global war on terror. Next came a campaign to convince U.S. public opinion that Saddam Hussein and Osama bin Laden were allies in their war against America. An alleged secret meeting in Prague in April 2001 between Mohamed Atta — the lead suicide bomber on September 11 — and an Iraqi intelligence agent got the ball rolling. Since then stories about the Saddam-al Qaeda nexus have become a cottage industry.

Bin Laden clearly hopes to use a U.S. invasion of a Muslim country to recruit thousands more to his cause. But the Saddam-bin Laden nexus was barely Step One in the Bush-Sharon Doctrine. The strategic objective is the antithesis of Middle Eastern stability.

The destabilization of "despotic regimes" comes next. In the Arab bowling alley, one ball aimed at Saddam is designed to achieve a 10-strike that would discombobulate authoritarian and/or despotic regimes in Iran, Syria, Saudi Arabia and the other Gulf Emirates and sheikhdoms.

The roots of the overall strategy can be traced to a paper published in 1996 by the Institute for Advanced Strategic and Political Studies, an Israeli think tank. The document was titled "A Clean Break: A New Strategy for Securing the Realm" and was designed as a political blueprint for the incoming government of Benjamin Netanyahu, a superhawk in the Israeli political aviary.

Israel, according to the 1996 paper, would "shape its strategic environment," beginning with the removal of Saddam Hussein and the restoration of the Hashemite monarchy in Baghdad. The Iraqi monarchy was overthrown in a military coup in 1958 when young King Faisal, a cousin of Jordan's late King Hussein, was assassinated.

The strategic roadmap—which has been followed faithfully thus far by both Mr. Netanyahu and his successor Mr. Sharon —called for the abandonment of the Oslo accords "under which Israel has no obligations if the PLO does not fulfill its obligations." Yasser Arafat blundered by obliging Israel.

"Our claim to thé land [of the West Bank] — to which we have clung for 2,000 years — is legitimate and noble," the paper continued. "Only the unconditional acceptance by Arabs of our rights, especially in their territorial dimension, is a solid basis for the future."[93]

And what is notable is that Israel's "strategic roadmap" referred to by deBorchgrave (and also referenced by Kaiser) was not just the product of an Israeli institution alone. The authors, as pointed out by Kaiser, were Americans—namely Richard Perle, Douglas Feith, John R. Bolton, and David Wurmser, all key "neo-conservative" policy makers guiding the Bush administration.

OPINION IN ISRAEL . . .

While all of this may have been a "revelation" to readers of *The Washington Post* and *The Washington Times*—which generally vary only by degree in pandering to the policy demands of the Israeli lobby in Washington, it was no surprise to the people of Israel.

Just two (of many) representatives reports in the Israeli press that noted comments by Israeli leaders demonstrates that the motivations of the "neo-conservative" policy makers were indeed part of a grand design very much in sync with Israel's fanatic Likud bloc:

> . . . "In the [occupied] territories, the Arab world, and in Israel, Bush's support for Sharon is being credited to the pro-Israel lobby, meaning Jewish money and the 'Christian' right."
>
> —Israeli writer Akiva Eldar, *Ha'aretz*, April 26, 2002

> "Sharon is finding it hard to show any achievements during his 20 months in power . . . an American attack on Iraq is seen as the lever which can extricate Israel from its economic, security and social quagmire . . . ."
>
> —Israeli correspondent Aluf Benn, *Ha'aretz*,
> November 18, 2002

Despite all this, the one independent American newspaper that has consistently dared to criticize the "neo-conservatives" and the Israeli lobby for Israel and to focus on their activities—*American Free Press*—was perhaps less circumspect than the "big name" elite publications such as *The Washington Post* and *The Washington Times* in summarizing the new alliance of the Bush administration with the Sharon regime.

BUSH POLICY—"GREATER ISRAEL"

Long before the major Washington dailies enunciated the Bush-Sharon alliance, *American Free Press* stated flatly that the Bush policies were part of a plan to establish the Zionist dream of a "Greater Israel." According to the report from *American Free Press*:

In league with the fanatic force of militant imperial Zionism, Big Oil was planning an all-out offensive to grab control of the oil riches of the entire Middle East. The international Anglo-American oil companies dream of shedding their partners in the oil rich Arab dynasties that control the oil fields. The oil barons want the oil all to themselves. At the same time, Zionist fanatics—both Christian and Jewish—dream of dismantling the Arab states and expanding Israel's borders to a "Greater Israel" reaching "From the Nile to the Euphrates."

With such a convergence of interests—based on a deadly mixture of ideology, profits and geopolitical power—Zionism and Big Oil had found common ground. As such, they were now moving to establish a Middle East hegemon over the oil riches of the Arab world. The campaign against Iraq was simply the opening gun.

The fact that the other Arab states of the Middle East had firmly declared their opposition to the proposed U.S. assault on Iraq set these states up as other enemies to be dispatched. The age-old Zionist aspiration for a "Greater Israel" is now no more than a cover for the oil conglomerates to seize absolute control of Arab oil, once and for all. The first step was eliminating Saddam Hussein.

Iraq is just the first domino slated to fall. The other Arab states are next in line. Knocking out the ruling Arab regimes will satisfy the demands of Israel's hard-liners, but also set the stage for the oil conglomerates to control Middle East oil.

It is no accident that the administration of George W. Bush should be the engine to achieve this goal. The scion of a family long a part of the intrigues of the Anglo-American oil elite, Bush—like his father—has been both allied with Israel and, when the circumstances required, standing in opposition to the Zionist state.

American Free Press pointed out that in the book *Friends In Deed: Inside the U.S.-Israel Alliance*, Israeli-based writers Dan Raviv and Yossi Melman wrote frankly of Israel's hostility to the senior Bush during his one-term in office—a point of which few Americans are aware, even including many stalwart Republican admirers of the Bush family.

As such, the Israelis have little trust for the family Bush. However, a Bush is in the White House in control of America's military arsenal. Israel recognizes American military power is the only thing that can assure Israel's survival in a world increasingly hostile to Israel's aims. Thus,

Bush and his allies in Big Oil find an alliance with Israel a necessity.

Zionist influence in American affairs—particularly in the realm of media control—has reached a zenith. In addition, the pro-Israel "Christian Right"—dominated by the likes of Jerry Falwell, Pat Robertson, Tim LaHaye, etc—is extremely influential in Republican Party ranks, positioning Bush's GOP base firmly in Israel's camp. At the same time, ironically, Israel's position has never been so precarious.

However—fortuitously, for Israel—the events of Sept. 11 brought the uneasy alliance between political Zionism and the plutocratic Big Oil forces full circle. As former CIA analyst George Friedman—a supporter of Israel—put it early on Sept. 11 on his widely cited website, www.stratfor.com, just hours after the tragic attacks: "The big winner today, intended or not, is the state of Israel."

Junior Bush has driven American military forces into the heart of the Arab world, to establish a geopolitical consortium in which U.S. military might can be used to "tame" the Arabs and grab control of their oil. In so doing Bush has the full propaganda might of the Zionist-dominated media behind him.

Open Secrets by the late Israeli scholar and critic of Zionism, Israel Shahak, frankly exposes Israel's foreign policy as a menace to world peace. Shahak contends it is a myth that there is any real difference between the supposedly "conflicting" policies of Israel's "opposing" Likud and Labor blocs, both of which advocate expansion aiming toward consolidating "Eretz Israel"—an imperial state in control of practically the entire Middle East. Israel, he asserts, is a militarist state: its policies are dictated by fundamentalist religious fanatics who now dominate Israel's military and intelligence elite.

If American forces destroy Saddam and occupy Iraq, *American Free Press* predicted, Israel would be a key partner in the consortium, by virtue of Israel's influence in Washington and over the media. Occupation of Iraq—even installation of a puppet regime—would be effective expansion of Israel's borders, fulfilling a considerable portion of the dream of "Greater Israel." *But at what cost to the American people?*

'CREATIVE DESTRUCTION' OF THE ARAB WORLD

Lest anyone chalk up these comments to "Arab paranoia," or "anti-Israel bigotry," note that one of Israel's most consequential advocates in official Washington—veteran pro-Israel intelligence community bureaucrat Michael Ledeen, a longtime close friend and associate of Richard Perle—has put out a propaganda screed titled *The War Against the Terror Masters* in which he writes of what he calls "creative destruction."

Ledeen says that this "creative destruction" is "entirely in keeping with American character and the American tradition"—an assertion that will surprise many Americans. Ledeen says that Iraq, Syria, Saudi Arabia and—for good measure—the non-Arabic Islamic Republic of Iran—should all be targets of "creative destruction" by U.S. military might.

"Creative destruction," writes Ledeen, is "our middle name,"—the term "our" referring to Americans, whether or not they share his imperialist views. According to Ledeen:

> We tear down the old order every day, from business to science, literature, art, architecture, and cinema to politics and the law.
>
> Our enemies have always hated this whirlwind of energy and creativity, which menaces their traditions (whatever they may be) and shames them for their inability to keep pace. Seeing America undo traditional societies, they fear us, for they do not wish to be undone.
>
> They cannot feel secure so long as we are there, for our very existence—our existence, not our policies—threatens their legitimacy. They must attack us in order to survive, just as we must destroy them to advance our historic mission.[94]

While his rhetoric is stilted and ponderous, what Ledeen is promoting is the idea that it is not U.S. support for Israel that engenders Arab hatred for the United States. Instead, he claims, it is the very existence of the United States—the "American way of life"—that inflames Arab passions. (What utter lies! What nonsense!)

Yet, these words are the propaganda line of the Israeli lobby which hopes to distract the attention of the American people away from the causes of Arab hostility to the United States stemming from unswerving U.S. support for Israel. Ledeen goes on to suggest that anyone who stands in opposition to all-out war against the Arab world needs to be removed from positions of authority. He writes:

> The president has to rid himself of those officials who failed to lead their
> agencies effectively, along with those who lack the political will to wage war
> against the terror masters.
>
> The top people in the intelligence community need to be replaced, and those
> military leaders who tell the president that it can't be done, or they just aren't
> ready, or we need to do something else first, should be replaced as well, along
> with the people in the national security community who insisted that we must
> solve the Arab-Israeli question before the war can resume and the top people in
> agencies like the FAA, the INS, and so forth.[95]

In fact, aside from other political considerations, President George W. Bush had good personal reason to do the bidding of the hard-line hawks in promoting their imperial schemes on behalf of Israel.

In the Feb. 1992 edition of *The Washington Report on Middle East Affairs*, former Rep. Paul Findley (R-Ill.) revealed that in 1991 former Israeli intelligence officer Victor Ostrovsky had blown the whistle on a plot by a right-wing faction within Israel's Mossad to kill then-President George H. W. Bush who was perceived as a threat to Israel.

After Ostrovsky provided the details to another former member of Congress, Pete McCloskey (R-Calif.), McCloskey conveyed a warning to the U.S. Secret Service. In his 1994 book, *The Other Side of Deception*, Ostrovsky revealed the specifics of what he had learned of the plot: the Mossad planned to assassinate Bush during an international conference in Madrid.

The Mossad had captured three Palestinian "extremists" and leaked word to the Spanish police that the terrorists were on their way to Madrid. The plan was to kill Bush, release the "assassins" in the midst of the confusion—and kill the Palestinians on the spot. The crime would be blamed on the Palestinians—another Mossad "false flag."

So it is that the George W. Bush administration is now fostering and nurturing the ancient dream of a Greater Israel. But to achieve that aim, the neo-conservative Zionist elements that achieved power in the Bush administration began laying the groundwork many years before. An initial step in that scheme was the enunciation of a theory known as "rogue states rollback."

"ROGUE STATES ROLLBACK" PART OF THE PLAN

A close study of the war-mongering policies of the neo-conservatives would not be complete without an examination of the policy of "rogue state rollback"—a plan, originating at the highest levels of the Zionist lobby in America—that has now seen the first drive toward its fulfillment.

"Rogue states" is an inflammatory term that has been used by Israel and its lobby in America—as well as by those who tout the imperialist propaganda line—to describe such largely Islamic countries as Iran, Iraq, Libya, Syria, Sudan, Afghanistan, and other countries that are perceived as threats to Israel. However, in light of current claims that the moderate oil-rich regime in Saudi Arabia is somehow "supporting terrorism," it can only be concluded that the neo-conservative war-mongers likewise consider the Saudi kingdom a "rogue" state as well.

The war against "rogue states" is all part of the effort to set in place a "new world order" in which no nation can retain its national sovereignty in the face of American military might held in the hands of a war-like "Israel-centric" combine of influence at the highest levels of the American government and supported by the major media.

A leading advocate of "rogue states rollback" is Sen. John McCain who, during his bid for the 2000 Republican presidential nomination, declared that as president, he would launch an all-out effort to destroy the "rogue" states.

What McCain didn't tell people was that "his" policy was, in fact, part of a long-range plan by higher-ups in the international policy-making elite, specifically the hard-line supporters of Israel.

This plan for "rogue states rollback"—then specifically targeting Iraq and Iran—was first enunciated on May 22, 1993 in a then-secret speech by a former Israeli government propagandist, Martin Indyk before the Washington Institute on Near East Affairs, a private, pro-Israel pressure group. At the time, the small, maverick American newspaper, *The Spotlight*, was the only publication to reveal this plan for aggression.

What made Indyk's strategic plan for war so explosive was that when Indyk outlined the policy, he was serving as President Clinton's hand-picked Middle East policy "expert" on the National Security Council.

Born in England and raised in Australia, Indyk took up residence in

Israel but was later given "instant" U.S. citizenship by special proclamation of President Clinton just hours after Clinton was sworn into office on Jan. 20, 1993—one of Clinton's first official acts. (Later this former Israeli propagandist was appointed to serve as U.S. ambassador to Israel, his obvious conflict of interest notwithstanding.)

Within a year, the thrust of Indyk's plan for war against Iraq and Iran was formally promoted by the powerful New York-based Council on Foreign Relations. It was also publicly announced, at the same time, as an official policy of the Clinton administration (although it had been in the making for over a year).

An Associated Press report, published in the Feb. 28, 1994 issue of *The Washington Post*, announced that W. Anthony Lake, President Clinton's National Security Advisor, had laid out a plan for "dual containment" of Iraq and Iran, both of which Lake labeled "outlaw" and "backlash" states.

Lake's comments as reported were from an article by Lake just published in the March/April 1994 issue of *Foreign Affairs*, the quarterly journal of the Rockefeller-financed Council on Foreign Relations (CFR), an American affiliate of the London-based Royal Institute for International Affairs, a policy group funded by the European Rothschild family, longtime supporters of Israel.

On Oct, 30, 1993, *The Washington Post* frankly described the CFR as "the nearest thing we have to a ruling establishment in the United States," saying that they are "the people who, for more than half a century, have managed our international affairs and our military-industrial complex,"[96] noting that 24 top members of the Clinton administration—along with Clinton—were CFR members.

There was a minor difference in the policy as set forth by Lake: Iraq was first targeted for destruction. Iran would come later.

Lake said the Clinton administration supported Iraqi exiles who wanted to overthrow Iraqi leader Saddam Hussein. Lake said that although Iran was what he called "the foremost sponsor of terrorism and assassination worldwide," the Clinton administration saw the possibility of better relations with Iran.

GINGRICH AND ISRAEL

In early 1995 the then-newly-elected Republican House Speaker, Newt Gingrich, long a vocal advocate for Israel, gave a little-noticed speech in Washington before a gathering of military and intelligence officers calling for a Middle East policy that was, in his words, "designed to force the replacement of the current regime in Iran . . . the only long-range solution that makes any sense."

That the then-de facto leader of the "opposition" Republican Party endorsed this policy was no real surprise since, at that time, Gingrich's wife was being paid $2,500 a month by the Israel Export Development Company, an outfit which lured American companies out of the United States into a high-tech business park in Israel.

Mrs. Gingrich was introduced to her employers when she was on a tour in Israel sponsored by the American-Israel Public Affairs Committee (AIPAC), a registered lobby for Israel.

A former AIPAC official, Arne Christensen, had served as a top policy advisor to Gingrich. Prior to his service for the Israeli lobby, Christensen had been on the staff of ex-Rep. Vin Weber (R-Minn.), a close Gingrich associate—and yet another member of the Council on Foreign Relations—who is, as noted previously, also one of the principals in William Kristol's "think tank" known as Empower America.

Weber later emerged as a top advisor to Sen. John McCain during his presidential campaign. And McCain is, yet again, also a CFR member. This perhaps helps explain how things came full circle and McCain promoted the line that the U.S. should take provocative measures against "rogue" states. *But the Israeli connection is what counts most . . .*

JOHN McCAIN—NEO-CONSERVATIVE SPOKESMAN

The Washington Post revealed on Feb. 25, 2000 that McCain included among his closest advisors three well-known pro-Israel commentators who are voices for what is indubitably the "Jewish Right"—figures in the so-called "neo-conservative" network: *New York Times* pundit William Safire, columnist Charles Krauthammer and the ubiquitous William Kristol, whose employer, fanatic pro-Israel media baron Rupert Murdoch, a satellite of the Rothschild family, endorsed McCain for president through the aegis of his daily, *The New York Post*.

McCain himself has declared his allegiance to Israel, above and beyond U.S. interests. In a March 14, 1999 speech in New York to the National Council of Young Israel, McCain said:

> We choose, as a nation, to intervene militarily abroad in defense of the moral values that are at the center of our national conscientiousness even when vital national interests are not necessarily at stake. I raise this point because it lies at the heart of this nation's approach to Israel. The survival of Israel is one of this country's most important moral commitments.

In short, McCain would be willing to commit the United States to a war in defense of Israel, even if U.S. "vital interests are not necessarily at stake." His endorsement of assaults upon the "rogue" Islamic states is part and parcel of this policy, which hardly places America first.

McCain has said that he is "driven" by "Wilsonian principles,"—the internationalist philosophy that U.S. military might should be used to enforce world standards, as dictated by the United States itself.

In fact, the record shows that McCain has long been part of an elite group promoting U.S. military action in defense of Israel. According to the Aug. 2, 1996 issue of the London-based *Jewish Chronicle*, McCain was a member of a little-known operation calling itself the Commission on America's National Interest that issued a report rating Israel as a "blue chip" interest for the United States worth "spending serious treasure and serious blood on,"—a conclusion many Americans might question.

The report ranked Israel's survival "on a par with preventing nuclear, biological and nuclear attacks on the U.S. as a vital American interest." The *Chronicle* summarized the report, quoting the group, with the head-line: "Americans 'should go to war to defend Israel.'"

Contrast this view with the results of a Sept. 1998 poll by the Pew Research Center for the People and the Press (reported in the Dec. 28, 1998 issue of *The Washington Post*) which found at the time that only 45 percent of the American public would support American intervention if Arab forces invaded Israel, compared with 74 percent of so-called "opinion elites" who would favor U.S. ground troops being committed to such a conflict. *But popular opinion in America apparently does not count.*

The war against "rogue" states and preparations for possible U.S.

military action to defend Israel was continually being hard-pressed in the
highest circles. It was clearly at the top of the elite's agenda.

NEO-CONSERVATIVES EXPAND THEIR TARGETS

On November 29, 1998, writing in *The Washington Post*, former
Secretary of State Henry Kissinger, a key CFR figure and longtime advocate for the Zionist cause, had a prominently placed article entitled "Bring
Saddam Down." More recently, however, the advocates of Israel began
expanding their targets.

In the March 2, 2000 issue of *The Washington Post*, columnist Jim
Hoagland wrote that there must be "a broad political and military strategy for the Persian Gulf . . . built around active U.S. support for representative democracy not only in Iraq and Iran but also in the conservative
Arab monarchies of the region. The two rogue states cannot be isolated as
the only candidates for change. . . ."

In other words, now even Arab states such as Saudi Arabia and perhaps the United Arab Emirates and Kuwait and others may face the wrath
of the imperialist "neo-conservative" elite, using the power of the
American military to achieve their goal.

Hoagland added that "U.S. policy on Iraq is a subject fit for campaign
debate [and that] . . . the candidate who can persuasively outline an inte-
grated political and military strategy to deal with the multiple national
security challenges of the gulf deserves serious consideration by
American voters."

In the end, although heavy-handed "rogue states rollback" advocate
John McCain did not achieve the presidency, his Republican primary
opponent, George W. Bush, did. And it was during the administration of
the new Republican president that the war against Iraq was launched—
culmination of a long-standing plan by the clique of "neo-conservatives"
whose well-financed, closely knit network had been planning just such a
move for nearly a generation.

THE OTHER 'AXIS OF EVIL'

Another key element in the push for an American imperium as advocated by the neo-conservative power bloc is the "axis of evil" between the neo-conservatives (whom, as we have seen, are largely hard-line Jewish hawks allied with the Sharon regime in Israel) and the so-called "Christian Right" in America—the hard-line dispensationalists.

Although journalist Jon Lee Anderson smirked in *The New Yorker* at what he called the "usual claims" by Iraqi deputy prime minister Tariq Aziz that, in Anderson's rendition of Aziz's remarks, "America had been hijacked by a small group of Jews and Christians, the oil lobby, and the military industrial complex,"[97] Aziz's allegations were on the mark.

While neither all American Jews nor all American Christians were allied with the neo-conservatives and the Christian fundamentalists in supporting the drive for a Greater Israel, Aziz was correct when he referred to a "small group" —influential though it may be.

The Christian Right, in fact, constitutes only a segment of the American Christian fundamentalist movement—although a large one to be sure. However, because the Christian Right has emerged as a key power base in the electoral ambitions of George W. Bush and the Republican Party, its influence on behalf of the neo-conservatives and the dream of a Greater Israel is beyond question.

Bush biographer Michael Lind believes that George W. Bush is personally driven toward acceptance of the neo-conservative doctrine precisely because of the fact that Bush seems to have abandoned his own family's traditional mainstream Christian religious convictions and adopted the same brand of Christian fundamentalism practiced by the hard-line Christian Right advocates of Israel.

Lind writes: "There is little doubt that the bonding between George W. Bush and Ariel Sharon was based on conviction, not expedience. Like the Christian Zionist base of the Republican Party, George W. Bush was a devout Southern fundamentalist."[98]

THE ASHCROFT CONNECTION

Although Bush has placed many neo-conservatives in powerful foreign policy making positions, we would be remiss in failing to mention his appointment of former Missouri Senator John Ashcroft—the member of a small but vocal fanatically pro-Israel Christian sect known as "the pentacostals"—as U.S. Attorney General. In that post Ashcroft is in charge of the entire American federal justice system and oversees the Federal Bureau of Investigation (the FBI), the federal law enforcement apparatus.

Although America's "liberal" special interest groups loudly protested Ashcroft's appointment, the fact is that while blacks, feminists, abortion advocates, homosexuals and others were cowering in fear at the prospect of John Ashcroft as attorney general, one particularly influential interest group—the pro-Israel lobby—had already given its "okay" to Ashcroft.

The first public sign of Israel's love for Ashcroft came when it was widely reported in the major media that Abe Foxman, national director of the Anti-Defamation League (ADL)—a powerful unit of the Israeli lobby—had announced that he expected Ashcroft to be a "just" man. Ashcroft supporters loudly touted Foxman's effective endorsement.

Meanwhile, those insiders who read *The New Republic* (TNR), a journal known as an influential and strident voice for the Israeli lobby, got the hint about Ashcroft's "acceptability" from a key source. Ashcroft's longtime policy director, Tevi Troy—an Orthodox Jew who once publicly referred to non-Jews as "goyim" (a racist term)—wrote an article (published in TNR issue on Jan. 29, 2001) promoting Ashcroft. Troy—now the Bush administration liaison to the Jewish community—said Ashcroft was "more than tolerant; he's downright philo-Semitic." Troy revealed:

> Ashcroft was born to a gentile family in a predominantly Jewish Chicago neighborhood. His mother served as a Shabbos goy [i.e. a non-Jew who works for Jews on the Jewish sabbath] turning ovens on and off as needed. Ashcroft's father even took a mezuzah [a Jewish religious symbol] with the family when they moved from Chicago to Springfield, Missouri, where he kept it affixed to his doorpost until his death, in 1995. Ashcroft, I'd wager, knows more about Judaism than half the Jewish members of the Senate.[99]

In the meantime, while liberal Jewish Democratic New York Sen. Charles Schumer was soothing his "liberal" constituents by publicly opposing Ashcroft, Schumer (like other insiders) knew full well that Ashcroft had been his (Schumer's) partner in introducing congressional measures in previous years designed to advance the interests of Israel. Among other things, Ashcroft and Schumer together:

• Co-sponsored a dangerous police-state style so-called "anti-terrorist" measure—strongly promoted by the ADL and the Israeli lobby—that grass-roots patriots across America rallied against and largely managed to bloc from total passage. This, of course, was *well before the 9-11 attacks.*

• Led efforts in Congress to force the transfer of the U.S. Embassy in Tel Aviv to Jerusalem; and

• Co-sponsored a measure to mandate U.S. opposition to any independent declaration of a Palestinian state.

For his vocal campaign against the Palestinians, the Institute for Public Affairs for the Union of Orthodox Jewish Congregations of America hailed Ashcroft as having "long been on record as a staunch supporter of the State of Israel and its safety and security."

AN ALLIANCE OF JEWISH AND CHRISTIAN EXTREMISTS . . .

Since assuming the post of attorney general, Ashcroft has indeed been a leading voice in favor of the neo-conservative Likud-style policies pursued by the administration, devotedly protecting Israel's interests. In the meantime, Ashcroft's neo-conservative allies in the Bush foreign policy apparatus have forged a powerful alliance with the Christian Right voting bloc. Former CIA analysts Bill and Kathleen Christison have described this phenomenon in particularly biting words:

> The dual loyalists in the Bush administration have given added impetus to the growth of a messianic strain of Christian fundamentalism that has allied itself with Israel in preparation for the so-called End of Days. These crazed fundamentalists see Israel's domination over all of Palestine as a necessary step toward fulfillment of the biblical Millennium, consider any Israeli relinquishment of territory in Palestine as a sacrilege, and view warfare between Jews and Arabs as a divinely ordained prelude to Armageddon.
>
> These right-wing Christian extremists have a profound influence on Bush and his administration, with the result that the Jewish fundamentalists working for the perpetuation of Israel's domination in Palestine and the Christian fundamentalists working for the Millennium strengthen and reinforce each other's policies in administration councils.

The Armageddon that Christian Zionists seem to be actively promoting and that Israeli loyalists inside the administration have tactically allied themselves with raises the horrifying but very real prospect of an apocalyptic Christian-Islamic war.

The neo-conservatives seem unconcerned, and Bush's occasional *pro forma* remonstrations against blaming all Islam for the sins of Islamic extremists do nothing to make this prospect less likely.

These two strains of Jewish and Christian fundamentalism have dovetailed into an agenda for a vast imperial project to restructure the Middle East, all further reinforced by the happy coincidence of great oil resources up for grabs and a president and vice president heavily invested in oil.

All of these factors—the dual loyalties of an extensive network of policy-makers allied with Israel, the influence of a fanatical wing of Christian fundamentalists, and oil—probably factor in more or less equally to the administration's calculations on the Palestinian-Israeli situation and on war with Iraq.

But the most critical factor directing U.S. policymaking is the group of Israeli loyalists: neither Christian fundamentalist support for Israel nor oil calculations would carry the weight in administration councils that they do without the pivotal input of those loyalists, who clearly know how to play to the Christian fanatics and undoubtedly also know that their own and Israel's bread is buttered by the oil interests of people like Bush and Cheney.

This is where loyalty to Israel by government officials colors and influences U.S. policymaking in ways that are extremely dangerous.[100]

THE HISTORY OF THE ALLIANCE . . .

One American Jewish historian, Benjamin Ginsberg, writing in his study, *The Fatal Embrace: Jews and the State*, has explored the role of the Christian Right's alliance with the neo-conservatives. He explains:

> Close relations between Israel and Christian fundamentalists began to develop after the conservative Likud bloc came to power in Israel in 1977, and strengthened after Reagan's presidential victory in the United States in 1980. After Reagan took office he received a telegraph signed by Reverend Jerry Falwell and other prominent Christian fundamentalist leaders urging him to give his full support to Israel which, they said, "from a religious, moral and strategic perspective," represented "our hopes for security and peace in the Middle East."
>
> The Begin government awarded Falwell the Zabotinsky Award for service to Israel and brought him and other leaders of the Christian right to Israel frequently as honored guests. Falwell strongly supported Israeli annexation of the occupied territories and moving the Israeli capital to Jerusalem. "There is no question

that Judea and Samaria should be part of Israel," Falwell declared. Moreover, "I believe that the Golan heights should be annexed as an integral part of the state of Israel," he said.[101]

Author Michael Lind suggests that Falwell may indeed be "the Likud Party's most important lobbyist in the United States."[102] In addition, as Jewish-American authors Ken Silverstein and Michael Scherer noted, Begin loved Falwell so much that he also presented Falwell with a Learjet for his efforts on behalf of Israel.[103]

THE NEO-CONSERVATIVES AND THE FUNDAMENTALISTS

Since Begin's time, subsequent Likud prime ministers built close ties with American evangelicals. According to Silverstein and Scherer:

> Christian conservatives provide Israel—and in particular the hard-line Likud Party of Prime Minister Ariel Sharon—with its most important political support in the United States. They oppose Israel ceding land to the Palestinians and are pressuring the Bush administration to close Palestinian offices in the United States. They also have close ties to GOP congressional leaders and to a group of high-ranking hawks in the Pentagon—led by Deputy Defense Secretary Paul Wolfowitz—that some DC insiders call the "Kosher Nostra." . . .
>
> They work to support Israel, ironically, because they believe it will lead to the ultimate triumph of Christianity. For them, the ongoing crisis in the Mideast has been prophesied in the Bible: After Jews reclaim the Holy Land, nonbelievers—including Jews and Muslims—will perish in Armageddon, and Jesus will return as the Messiah to lead his followers to Heaven.
>
> Indeed, thanks to the top-level connections and grassroots activism of evangelical Christians, U.S. policy in the Middle East has never been so closely aligned with Israel as it is under the administration of George W. Bush . . .[104]

The Christian evangelicals are particularly hard-hearted against Arabs and Muslims. They believe "that Arabs and Muslims can be traced back to Ishmael, the unfavored son of Abraham, who was promised by God vast land and resources but who would never be satisfied with what he had. No matter how much good fortune Arabs receive . . . they will never know spiritual peace,"[105] in the view of these Christian extremists. (And it should be noted that this is not the standard view of the typical American Christian, as we shall see.)

Pointing out that one of the hawks within the Bush administration

who has worked closely with the Christian right is Douglas Feith—the deputy to Deputy Defense Secretary Paul Wolfowitz—Silverstein and Scherer cite Feith's former associate at the Center for Security Policy, Frank Gaffney, who asserts: "You are seeing American government policy being profoundly influenced by beliefs that are shared by the pushers outside [the Christian evangelicals] and the people on the inside [the Jewish neo-conservatives]."[106]

Noting the enthusiastic reception by Israel's Likud of the fundamentalists, Michael Lind comments that "The fervent support of Israel by Protestant fundamentalists . . . has been manipulated for a quarter of a century by right-wing Israeli politicians and their neo-conservative allies."[107]

Ironically, however, even "liberal" American Jewish groups that do support Israel, but which publicly advocate a negotiated settlement with the Palestinians, see the danger in this unholy alliance between the Christian evangelicals and the Jewish neo-conservatives.

Rabbi Eric Yoffie, head of the Union of American Hebrew Congregations, is quoted as saying that this alliance of evangelicals and neo-conservatives sees "any concession as a threat to Israel, and in this way they strengthen the hardliners in Israel and the United States."[108]

THE FANATICS IN CONGRESS

In the U.S. Congress, there are a number of lawmakers who are closely aligned with the Christian fundamentalists and their Zionist warhawk allies. Notable among them are House Republican Majority Leader Tom DeLay of Texas who "agrees with hawkish Israelis that the West Bank and Golan Heights are part of Israel rather than occupied territories."[109]

In the Senate, one of the leading pro-Israel Christian "hawks" is Sen. Sam Brownback, a Kansas Republican. However, perhaps even more rhetorically and fanatically extreme than Brownback in terms of supporting the hard-line Likudniks—Christian and Jewish alike—is Sen. James Inhofe of Oklahoma, another member of the Republican Party.

Although on Election Night 2000, NBC's Tom Brokaw described Sen. James Inhofe (R-Okla.) as a "foreign policy expert," Inhofe's record of expertise seems more in the field of religious fanaticism of the Christian Zionist fundamentalist persuasion.

For example, on March 4, 2002, Inhofe said in a speech to the Senate that God allowed terrorists to attack the United States on Sept. 11, 2001 to punish America for being too tough on Israel. In a speech condemning his fellow Republican, President Bush, who then was perceived to be pressing too hard on Israel, Inhofe stated in no uncertain terms:

> One of the reasons I believe the spiritual door was opened for an attack against the United States of America is that the policy of our government has been to ask the Israelis, and demand it with pressure, not to retaliate in a significant way against the terrorist strikes that have been launched against them.[110]

Although American broadcast media had previously attacked speakers from the Muslim world who had suggested, in one fashion or another, that the Sept. 11 attack on the United States was the will of Allah, there was hardly a mention anywhere of Inhofe's inflammatory remarks.

Inhofe was not the only American Christian fundamentalist to make such a comment. On Oct. 11, 2002, evangelist Joyce Meyer told the Christian Coalition at its national conference that the American people deserved the 9-11 attack for failing to stand firmly with God on the side of Israel. "If we don't obey God, God's protection is lifted,"[111] she announced. Yet, the major media has ignored such pro-Israel insanity.

Inhofe has also sought to explain that the native Palestinians have never had a historical right to Palestine and that when they were there, they contributed little to the region.

For example, in another Senate speech Inhofe quoted the 18th century French philosopher Voltaire as describing the Palestine of his day as being a "hopeless dreary place." However, what Inhofe, in his bias in favor of the Jewish occupiers of Palestine seems to have ignored is what Voltaire is also reported to have said on another occasion: "While the Arabs are distinguished by courage, hospitality and humanity, the Jews are cowardly and lecherous, greedy and miserly."

The Oklahoma senator suggested that Palestine was a desolate area that no one wanted. "Where was this great Palestinian nation?" asked Inhofe. "It did not exist. It was not there. Palestinians were not there." While any normal individual with even the most minimal knowledge of the history of Palestine knows that Inhofe's claims are the product of a fevered imagination, the sorry fact is that many millions of Americans share those provocative and hateful views.

PRO-ZIONIST MEDIA PROMOTES FUNDAMENTALIST SECT

The truth is that the American media (long favorable to Israel) has helped advance the cause of the Christian Right and its "dispensationalist" followers who are so wedded to the "neo-conservative" cause in America and with its allies in Israel.

For example, quite notably, *Time*, the weekly newsmagazine, published by the AOL-Time Warner media mega-monopoly, recently emerged as a leading promoter of the "last days" philosophy of dispensationalism identified with Christian televangelists who are allied with the "neo-conservative" ruling clique inside the Bush administration.

In a lavishly illustrated July 1, 2002 cover story entitled "The Bible & The Apocalypse—Why more Americans are reading and talking about the end of the world," *Time* provided thirteen full pages of publicity for "end times" promoters—in particular, "conservative" Christian Right evangelist Tim LaHaye, an unlikely hero for a magazine usually identified as being a voice of the liberal persuasion.

Why the super-rich plutocrats who dominate AOL-*Time* Warner—including billionaire whiskey baron Edgar Bronfman, head of the World Jewish Congress—would use their media clout to promote a particular brand of Christian theology is a question that many American Christians who disagree with "dispensationalist" philosophy began asking.

The thirteen pages in the Bronfman family-dominated magazine featured 13 different brightly illustrated articles or sidebars or explanatory material. A great deal of effort was put into promoting LaHaye:

In the opening paragraph, the lead article trumpeted LaHaye's newest book, *The Remnant*, as "the biggest book of the summer" and featured a prominently-placed photo of the book's cover.

Across the top of various pages through the spread were such boxed "facts" cited as "36% of those polled who support Israel say they do so because they believe in biblical prophecies that Jews must control Israel before Christ will come again" or "42% say they support Israel because Jews are God's chosen people."

Four full pages in a single article focused specifically on LaHaye. A large and attractive two-page spread color photograph of a gesturing LaHaye, taken from below, making him appear almost towering, was accompanied by the title, in large letters, "Meet the Prophet." A second-ary photograph featured a smiling, casually dressed LaHaye being nuz-zled by his attractive wife and collaborator, Beverly, describing them as a "power couple" who "share an evangelical zeal."

In a side-bar to the LaHaye article, *Time* enthusiastically provided color photographs of:

• LaHaye's *Left Behind* comic-style "graphic novels"

• Lahaye's *Left Behind* board game,

• The covers of six of LaHaye's 22 children's books,

• LaHaye's *Left Behind* CDs (which *Time* advertises to its readers are audio versions "with some music"; and

• A still photo from the movie sequel to LaHaye's original *Left Behind* film extravaganza. Just so nobody missed the premiere, *Time* advised its readers that LaHaye's new film would be "due in November."

Few could be so lucky to get this kind of media attention! And clear-ly all of the aforementioned was valuable publicity that LaHaye would have otherwise had to spend millions to achieve. But there was more.

In the main article in the series, *Time*'s editors spread color photo-graphs—with capsule descriptions—of ten of LaHaye's "Left Behind" series of full-length novels across two pages, including yet a second pic-ture of LaHaye's newest novel, *The Remnant*, which had already been promoted and pictured in the first paragraph of the very same article.

Under each picture and capsule description of each novel, *Time* gen-erously cited the Biblical scripture on which each novel is purportedly based and, in large, bold type, bleated "Copies Sold 7,000,000" (or what-ever the relevant figure) under the illustration of each of the books.

Another article asked what was probably the pertinent question about LaHaye's dispensationalist viewpoint (as far as the Bronfman family is concerned): "Is it good for the Jews?" The answer, it seems, is "yes."

Although *Time* noted that some Jewish theologians are upset by the fact that LaHaye and the dispensationalists see the "end times" as the period when Jews must accept Jesus Christ as the messiah, *Time* left the critical final judgment to a leading voice of the pro-Israel lobby.

According to *Time*: "Yet when a people feels isolated and under attacks, it will take all the friends it can get, retorts Abraham Foxman, national director of the Anti-Defamation League." *Time* then quoted

Foxman directly: "I don't think it's our business to get at the heart and soul and metaphysics of people as to why they come to support Israel. Some do it for a national-interest point of view, some because of moral issues, some because of theological issues. We don't set standards or conditions for support." *So the Christian Right is Israel's right arm.*

THE PRO-ZIONIST MEDIA ATTACKS THE VATICAN

On the reverse side, the major media in America has done much to condemn Christian religious leaders and factions that raise questions about the neo-conservative War Party and its Christian Right adherents.

For example, Korean cult leader Sun Myung Moon—publisher of the neo-conservative-oriented *Washington Times*—aimed his newspaper's fire at the Roman Catholic Church and Pope John Paul II in the Vatican. Effectively confirming the charge made in 2002 by a Vatican-endorsed newspaper that the major media is hostile to the Catholic Church because of its opposition to U.S. aggression against Iraq, Moon's newspaper fired an editorial volley against the church for precisely that reason.

On January 22, 2003, Moon's *Washington Times* complained that "recent history suggests that a note of caution is in order when it comes to listening to the Catholic Church's warnings regarding U.S. military action against Iraq."[112]

Noting that the Vatican and Catholic leaders in the United States "have distinguished themselves in recent months as two of the sharpest critics of possible U.S. military strikes against Iraq, the *Times* pointed out that in the lead-up to the Persian Gulf War of 1991 that "the pope issued numerous statements questioning the wisdom of going to war."

That a self-styled "mainstream" newspaper would venture so far as to publish such an editorial might strike some critics as venturing into the arena of religious bigotry, inasmuch as those who have otherwise dared to suggest that perhaps "Jewish influence" has been a major force promoting U.S. involvement in a war against Iraq have been accused of "stoking the fires of religious hatred." However, the Moon newspaper seems to have no problem with attacking the Catholic Church and its leadership when they take a policy position differing from that of Reverend Moon and the pro-Israel contingency that dictates the overriding "neo-conservative" editorial policy of *The Washington Times.*

Moon's assault on the Vatican came as no surprise to those who were aware that in its June 1, 2002 issue, *Civilta Cattolica*—an influential journal sanctioned by the Vatican—had fired a shot at the American media for its obsessive coverage of the Catholic Church sex scandals. *Civilta Cattolica* flatly asserted that—at least in part because the Catholic Church refused to support the media-promoted war against Saddam in 1991 that the controllers of the American media had nursed a grudge against the church.

Given that—as the record indicates—the media's sudden and intense interest in the church's problems did, in fact, explode after Sept. 11, it is interesting to note that *Civilta Cattolica* also cited the aftermath of 9-11 in its dissection of the media's attacks on the church.

In fact, *Civilta Cattolica* suggested that the Catholic Church's appeals against "vendettas" against the Arab and Muslim world in the wake of 9-11 also offended the media, which has been heavily promoting an anti-Arab and anti-Muslim agenda, often quoting so-called "experts" on terrorism and on the Middle East who are—more often than not—advocates of Israeli policy and often directly affiliated with Israeli intelligence.

Now, *The Washington Times* came forward almost as if to confirm the weight of the Vatican-endorsed newspaper's charge.

LIEBERMAN FOR PRESIDENT?

What is of equal (and related) interest to note is that even as the *Times*—which is quite influential in Republican circles—was attacking the Vatican for its stance on the U.S.-Iraq conflict, the same newspaper was giving friendly nods to the Democratic presidential aspirations of Sen. Joseph Lieberman, hailing him as the kind of statesman Americans needed to support precisely because of his determination to draw the United States into a war against Iraq.

In 2001, in a lead editorial on Aug. 13—entitled "A Scoop Jackson Democrat"—the *Times* praised Lieberman's front-line role in the ongoing effort to spark a U.S. invasion of Iraq. According to the *Times*:

> When it comes to understanding the most important foreign policy issues of the day—in particular, the need to explain to the American public why President Bush is right to forge ahead with plans to overthrow Iraqi ruler Saddam Hussein—Mr. Lieberman is providing exactly the right kind of leadership.[113]

The *Times* asserted that "It is no exaggeration to say that Mr. Lieberman's longstanding approach to foreign policy issues is much like the one taken by the late Sen. Henry 'Scoop' Jackson of Washington during the Cold War."[114]

The comparison is probably no coincidence considering the fact that the real "brains" behind Jackson's hawkish (and vehemently pro-Israel) stance was none other than Richard Perle, now the chief ideologue among the "neo-conservative" war hawks who orchestrated the war against Iraq. During Jackson's heyday, Perle was Jackson's chief behind-the-scenes advisor, steering the otherwise "liberal" Jackson into a confrontational stance against the then-Soviet Union, primarily because of the fact that the Kremlin—at that time—was being accused of being "anti-Zionist."

The *Times'* endorsement of Lieberman recalls the effusive praise that Rev. Jerry Falwell—another fanatic supporter of Israel and leading Republican—gave Lieberman during the 2000 campaign when Lieberman was Al Gore's vice presidential running mate.

Although a bizarre figure, the *Times'* publisher—Moon—has long been entangled with hard-line "neo-conservative" elements of the American lobby for Israel. As a consequence, that Moon's newspaper should promote Lieberman's call for war (and his candidacy) at the same time it was attacking the Vatican for opposing the war is thus no surprise.

CHRISTIAN CRITICS OF PRO-ZIONIST FANATICISM

On the positive side, it should be noted that there is a Christian reaction in America against the "end times" advocates of Israel who are allied with the "neo-conservatives." While there has always been a mainstream group of Christian fundamentalists who have loudly and consistently questioned the very concept of "dispensationalism," arguing with the pro-Israel advocates over the idea that the modern-day state of Israel constitutes the Israel of the Bible—a thesis that they reject—this group has been largely low-key, fearing the wrath of the American media which is quick to charge critics of Israel with "anti-Semitism."

However, in the Washington, DC area, for many years, a well-known Christian evangelist named Dale Crowley, Jr. has regularly broadcast a six-times weekly radio forum (over WFAX-AM 1220) in which he takes to task the Israeli lobby, its neo-conservative operatives and the Christian Right figures with whom the neo-conservatives are allied.

Recently Crowley penned an "Open Letter to Jerry Falwell," published in the national weekly newspaper, *American Free Press*, which harshly condemned Falwell and his fellow-travelers in the Christian Right for their support for Israeli aggression against the Palestinian Muslims and the Palestinian Christians.

A devout Christian in the traditional fundamentalist mode, Crowley has often faced the wrath of the Anti-Defamation League (ADL) of B'nai B'rith for his outspoken voice, but he remains undaunted.

Yet another Washington, DC area Christian activist, E. Stanley Rittenhouse, has likewise energetically posed a challenge to Falwell and the pro-Zionist elements. On one occasion Rittenhouse organized a picket line outside Falwell's church, hoping to convince Falwell's followers of the dangers blind alliance to Zionism and Israeli imperialism pose both to America and to Christian tradition.

A fascinating book by Rittenhouse, *For Fear of the Jews*, is a well-written exposition on the topic that pulls no punches.

One of the nation's best known Christian critics of the evangelical alliance with Zionism is Oregon-based Rev. Theodore Winston "Ted" Pike who—with his wife Alynn—has produced several remarkable videos, including *The Other Israel*, *Why the Mid-East Bleeds*, and *Zionism & Christianity: Unholy Alliance*, each of which addresses various aspects of the Middle East crisis and are highly recommended.

In addition, there is a growing body of other Christians—who are operating largely independent of the organized churches—who also reject dispensationalism and who openly criticize the leading evangelists such as Falwell, Pat Robertson, Tim LaHaye and others. These are the so-called "Preterists" who contend (based on solid historical fact) that modern-day dispensationalism is hardly traditional Christian teaching at all and is largely based on a theory popularized in the early 20th century by one Cyrus Scofield. The Preterists charge that Scofield's dispensationalism was actively promoted and funded by the Rothschild family of Europe for the very purpose of advancing the Zionist cause and for fostering a push for an imperial global order quite similar indeed to the policies being pursued by the "neo-conservative" elements in the Bush administration in alliance with the Christian Right.

Among the more prominent of the Preterists are such figures as Don
K. Preston and John Anderson who have been producing a wide array of
literature and videos challenging the dispensationalist teachings and
propaganda. Another is Syrian-born Christian scholar Robert Boody, now
a proud citizen of America, who has been a forthright critic not only of
the dispensationalists but also of the stridently pro-Israel and anti-Arab
tendencies of the American government.

The outreach of the Preterists to many American Christians is succeeding to the point that the leaders of the dispensationalist movement—
such as Tim LaHaye—are energetically working to combat this increasingly influential message.

So it is that while the Christian Right and its "Likudnik" allies among
the neo-conservatives are now in a position of power, there is a growing
rebellion among the ranks of good American Christians who do not
believe in war and destruction aimed against the Arab and Muslim world
on behalf of Zionist imperialism under whatever guise it may mask itself.

THE AMERICAN-ISRAELI 'TERRORISM INDUSTRY'

The American media not only promotes the Christian and Jewish
extremist alliance that supports the "neo-conservative" network, but it
also lends its considerable clout to efforts by the neo-conservatives to turn
Americans against the Arab and Muslim world.

For many years—long before the 9-11 terrorist attacks—the
American media has broadcast fears of "terrorism" with the message
clear: Arabs are terrorists, or, at the least, potential terrorists.

In fact, as the record shows, when the media turns to "experts" for
information about terrorism, more often than not they're turning to
sources with close ties to Israel and its American lobby.

In 1989, Pantheon Books published a little-noticed volume that pro-
vides a stark and revealing look at the development and growth of what
the authors dubbed "the terrorism industry."

In *The "Terrorism" Industry: The Experts and Institutes That Shape
Our View of Terror,* Professor Edward Herman of the University of
Pennsylvania and his co-author, Gerry O'Sullivan, have provided a com-
prehensive and scholarly overview of the way that powerful private spe-

cial interests (both foreign and domestic) have worked together with government agencies in the United States and internationally to influence the way that the world looks upon the phenomenon of modern-day terrorism.

Although the authors do not focus exclusively on the role of Israel and its American lobby in the "terrorism industry," it is very clear from their carefully documented findings that Israel does indeed constitute a major player and has, from the very beginning.

THE KRISTOL CONNECTION—YET AGAIN

According to the authors: "Many of the institutes and think tanks that are important components of the terrorism industry originated or grew rapidly as part of a major corporate offensive in the 1970s."[115]

They point out that one of the key organizers and fund-raisers—a powerful public relations voice behind this corporate offensive—was Irving Kristol who "succeeded in mobilizing a wide array of wealthy individuals, firms and foundations in the overall funding enterprise." Kristol, of course, is the father of William Kristol, the primary publicist for the ideology of the "neo-conservative" network.

Using his clout within the ranks of the elite, it was the senior Kristol who was thus one of the prime movers behind a growing number of institutions devoting their resources to the study of "terrorism"—at least as Kristol and his associates define it.

So the "war against terrorism" was part and parcel of the neo-conservative long-range view—well before 9-11.

THE ISRAELI CONNECTION—YET AGAIN

In *The 'Terrorism' Industry*, Herman and O'Sullivan have pointed out the Israeli connections of some of the more notable institutions known for their active engagement in analyzing and explaining terrorism:

• The neo-conservative Heritage Foundation "helps fund and engages in joint activities with institutes in Great Britain and Israel."

• The Jewish Institute on National Security Affairs (JINSA) "was organized and is run by individuals closely tied to the Israeli lobby and can be regarded as a virtual agency of the Israeli government."

• Georgetown University's Center for Strategic and International

Studies includes such well known "experts" on terrorism often quoted in the media as Michael Ledeen, Walter Laquer and Edward Luttwak who "have had very close relationships with Israel and Mossad."

• The Institute for Studies in International Terrorism at the State University of New York, has "extensive international ties to military police and intelligence operations as well as the U.S., European, and Israeli right [which] reflect [founder Yonah] Alexander's own connections."

THE MEDIA PROMOTES THE 'TERRORISM INDUSTRY'

With these institutions and others feeding "facts" about terrorism to the public, the media falls down on the job, according to Herman and O'Sullivan, by accepting without question the information (or is it "disinformation"?) on terrorism that the terrorism industry puts forth:

"The terrorism industry produces the Western 'line' on terrorism, and selects the appropriately supportive 'facts,' and the mass media disseminate these to the public. The transmission process is smooth, as the mass media pass long the manufactured messages without further substantial processing, functioning essentially as conduits.

"The U.S. mass media have raised no questions about the premises and agenda of the terrorism industry and generally fail even to filter out or correct literal error."

Herman and O'Sullivan cite, as one example, a four-part series on "counter-terrorism" that appeared in *The New York Times* on December 2, 3, 4, and 5, 1984. The authors point out that the *Times* relied on Israeli officials and experts for about 20% of the information disclosed. The balance of those interviewed were largely U.S. officials and other "experts," but the authors did not indicate whether the U.S. officials and experts included in the *Times* report had ties to Israel and its American lobby.

STATE-SPONSORED TERRORISM FOR POLITICAL AIMS

The authors indicate, based upon their findings, that there is good reason to believe that certain acts of "terrorism" are, in fact, deliberate provocations created to advance the agenda of those ostensibly fighting terrorism. They write:

Agents of the state, and those of private groups as well, may not only implicate terrorists from within terrorist organizations, they may urge them to commit terrorist acts to justify prosecution. They themselves may carry out terrorist acts—attributed to others—for propaganda purposes. We believe that these actions are of great and underestimated importance.

It is not difficult for agents of intelligence organizations to set off a bomb or even to kill individuals, or to encourage or hire others to do these things; then to make a phone call claiming responsibility on behalf of a Red network or Palestinian organization. This is an easy way of creating a desired moral environment, and there is substantial evidence that states have frequently engaged in such practices.

The Israeli government carried out a number of terrorist bombings of U.S. facilities in Cairo in 1955-56, hoping that these would be attributed to Egyptians and damage relations between Egypt and the United States. In the United States, the FBI has long engaged in agent provocateur actions, urging violence on penetrated dissident organizations and carrying out direct acts of violence, then attributed to the individuals and organizations under attack.

There is much more to the business of "terrorism" than meets the eye, as Herman and O'Sullivan have pointed out. For this reason, Americans especially need to be wary of media reports about "terrorism" and to carefully consider precisely who is behind such reports.

STEVEN EMERSON—DISINFORMATION SPECIALIST

One particular terrorism "expert" often cited by the media is worth examining. He is Steven Emerson—reportedly Jewish, although he will not acknowledge it, at least publicly—who is frequently featured in the media in America.

Critics have called him a "fanatic Arab and Muslim hater," which he clearly is. One independent journalist, John Sugg, has summarized Emerson's activities, pointing out his Israeli connections:

A closer look at Emerson's career suggests his priority is not so much news as it is an unrelenting attack against Arabs and Muslims . . .

Emerson gained prominence in the early 90s. He published books, wrote articles, produced a documentary, won awards and was frequently quoted. The media, Capitol Hill and scholars paid attention . . .

As Emerson's fame mounted, so did criticism. Emerson's book, *The Fall of Pan Am 103*, was chastised by *The Columbia Journalism Review*, which noted in

July 1990 that passages "bear a striking resemblance, in both substance and style" to reports in *The Post-Standard* of Syracuse, N.Y. Reporters from the Syracuse newspaper told this writer that they cornered Emerson at an Investigative Reporters and Editors conference and forced an apology.

A *New York Times* review (5/19/91) of his 1991 book *Terrorism* chided that it was "marred by factual errors...and by a pervasive anti-Arab and anti-Palestinian bias." His 1994 PBS video, *Jihad in America* (11/94), was faulted for bigotry and misrepresentations—veteran reporter Robert Friedman (*The Nation*, 5/15/95) accused Emerson of "creating mass hysteria against American Arabs." ... "He's poison," says investigative author Seymour Hersh, when asked about how Emerson is perceived by fellow journalists ...

[Emerson] scored a November 1996 hit in *The Pittsburgh Tribune-Review* (11/3/96)—owned by right-wing Clinton-basher Richard Mellon Scaife, who also partially funded *Jihad in America*.

Considering Scaife's patronage, it is not surprising that Emerson declared that Muslim terrorist sympathizers were hanging out at the White House. Emerson had a similar commentary piece printed three months earlier in *The Wall Street Journal* (8/5/96), one of the writer's few consistent major outlets ...

As recognition of Emerson's liabilities has grown, he has handed his bullhorn to less controversial fellow travelers. Retired federal agents Oliver "Buck" Revell and Steve Pomerantz, who run a security business, showed up echoing Emersonisms in an October 31 *Washington Post* article warning of conspiracies and front organizations . . .

Revell also acknowledges another member of the fraternity is Yigal Carmon, a right-wing Israeli intelligence commander who endorsed the use of torture (*Washington Post*, 5/4/95), and who has stayed at Emerson's Washington apartment on trips to lobby Congress against Middle East peace initiatives (*The Nation*, 5/15/95).

Says Vince Cannistraro, an ABC consultant and a retired CIA counterterrorism official, of Emerson's allies, Pomerantz, Revell and Carmon: "They're Israeli-funded. How do I know that? Because they tried to recruit me." Revell denies Cannistraro's assertion, but refuses to discuss his group's finances.

Emerson's own financing is hazy. He has received funding from Scaife. Some Emerson critics suspect Israeli backing. *The Jerusalem Post* (9/17/94) has noted that Emerson has "close ties to Israeli intelligence."

"He's carrying the ball for Likud," says investigative journalist Robert Parry, referring to Israel's right-wing ruling party. Victor Ostrovsky, who defected from Israel's Mossad intelligence agency and has written books disclosing its secrets, calls Emerson "the horn"—because he trumpets Mossad claims.[116]

THE 'GRANDFATHER' OF ANTI-ARAB FANATICISM

Emerson, however, is not the only widely-touted media darling reported to be an "expert" on terrorism and the Arab world. More prominent than Emerson—and certainly more widely "respected" in the classic sense—is aging Princeton University Professor Bernard Lewis.

Although Lewis is Jewish and although his son is active in AIPAC, the lobby for Israel in Washington, these two details are seldom—if ever—mentioned by the media which gives Lewis great fanfare and promotes his books and lectures, including, most particularly, his recent book, *What Went Wrong*, a vicious attack on the history of the Arab and Muslim peoples. In fact, Lewis is very much a much-heralded voice—however biased—for the neo-conservative movement.

Delving into what the author describes as "the warped world of Bernard Lewis," Anis Shivani has summarized Lewis's Arab- and Muslim-hating worldview:

> Lewis was the one who originally coined the odious term, "clash of civilizations," in his supercilious *Atlantic Monthly* article of September 1990, "The Roots of Muslim Rage." This article appeared after the fall of the Berlin Wall and preparatory to identifying the new enemy.
>
> In that article, Lewis rejects all the obvious explanations—failures of American policy, for instance—and looks for "something deeper" that "makes every problem insoluble," without identifying what that something deeper could be. He dismisses imperialism as an explanation for "rage" and "humiliation," suggesting that anti-imperialism has a [Muslim] religious connotation.
>
> In books like *The Arabs in History* (1950), *The Emergence of Modern Turkey* (1961), *Semites and Anti-Semites* (1986), *The Jews of Islam* (1984), and *Islam and the West* (1993) Lewis has catalogued what he sees as the incurable pathologies of the Islamic world in its suspended state of humiliation.[117]

Ironically, Shivani points out that despite his reputation as a wide-ranging scholar, Lewis' premise is based on quite a limited foundation in the first place:

> In his new book, Lewis opens his account of "what went wrong" with the beginning of Ottoman military setbacks in the sixteenth and later centuries. Lewis's interpretation of Islam is heavily Ottomancentric, hardly dealing with the substance of South Asian, Southeast Asian, Central Asian, Persian or North

African civilization, and yet he extrapolates to the whole world of Islam through all of time.[118]

Noting Lewis's profound propensity for dismissing all of the accomplishments and remarkable history of the Arab and Muslim worlds, Shivani concludes:

> This is the template according to which Americans are being prepared for a final onslaught against those foolish enough to think that there could be an alternative to the American model.
>
> All previous Muslim attempts to modernize have only increased the power of the state to tyrannize; the conclusion is that we should take away their power and leave them pauperized.[119]

Despite Lewis' obvious bias—or perhaps because of it—Lewis has been a key behind-the-scenes player in impacting Bush administration policies that led up to the assault on Iraq. On April 5, 2003 *The New York Times* described Lewis's inflammatory book, *What Went Wrong*, as having been a major influence on Bush administration thinking, particularly that of Vice President Dick Cheney.

BERNARD LEWIS & THE IMPERIAL DREAM

The *Times* also revealed that even prior to the 9-11 terrorist attacks Lewis was a key participant in a little-known study—sponsored by Defense Secretary Donald Rumsfeld and his deputy, Paul Wolfowitz— that examined ancient empires, in order "to understand how they maintained their dominance."[120]

Notably, the *Times* did not rush to explain to its American readers why officials of their government—a regime faced with many internal problems at home ranging from illiteracy, unemployment, declining infrastructure, poverty and disease—would be concerned with the historical day-to-day machinations of ancient empires.

However, the fact that Lewis was called in to advise on such a topic indicates the direction in which the "neo-conservatives" were heading, long before the seemingly convenient 9-11 tragedy that gave them the pretext upon which to act.

Lest there be any doubt that Lewis's point of view is only one of many points of view considered by the Bush administration, note what the

Bush administration's chief "neo-conservative" imperialist ideologue, Paul Wolfowitz said admiringly of Lewis via satellite during a tribute to Lewis held in Israel:

> Bernard Lewis has brilliantly placed the relationships and the issues of the Middle East into their larger context, with truly objective, original—and always independent—thought. Bernard has taught [us] how to understand the complex and important history of the Middle East and use it to guide us where we will go next to build a better world for generations.[121]

Lamis Andoni, a veteran journalist who has covered the Middle East for some 20 years for a wide variety of publications, has provided a particularly valuable overview of Lewis's career as an advocate for the new imperialism. Ms. Andoni noted that "Lewis has not only provided historical justification for Washington's 'war on terror,' but has also emerged as chief ideologue for the re-colonization of the Arab world through an American invasion of Iraq."[122] Ms. Andoni encapsulates Lewis's dubious contribution to international friendship and cooperation:

> Lewis's work, especially his book *What Went Wrong: Western Impact and Middle Eastern Response*, has been a major source in what is practically a manifesto for advocates of US military intervention towards "establishing democracy in the Middle East." By declaring that the peoples of the Middle East, meaning Arabs and Iranians, have failed to catch up with modernity and have fallen into "a downward spiral of hatred and rage," Lewis has at once exonerated American imperial policies and provided a moral imperative for President George W Bush's "preemptive strikes" and "regime change" doctrines.
>
> In fact, Lewis, according to published reports and his own statements, has been involved in lobbying, shaping and promoting the Bush Administration's most hawkish policies in support of Israel against the Palestinians, and for the aggressive use of American military force in the region.
>
> His influence is not merely a result of his academic stature and prolific writings on Islam, rather it is primarily a function of his membership in an alliance of neo-conservatives and hard-line Zionists who have come to assume key posts in the Bush administration.
>
> On February 19, [1998], representatives of the alliance, including Lewis, [future US Defense Secretary Donald] Rumsfeld [and his future Deputy Defense Secretary, Paul] Wolfowitz and others, signed a letter urging President Bill Clinton to launch a military offensive, which would have included blanket bombings, to destroy the Iraqi regime.
>
> Lewis provides "a scholarly" cover for a lobby that has been openly advo-

cating the reshaping of the regional map to eliminate "the Arab threat to Israel." Furthermore, Lewis considers Israel and Turkey the only real nation states in the region and has been forecasting the demise and the disintegration of Arab states since the Gulf War. Lewis, who worked for British intelligence during World War II, not only has considerable nostalgia for bygone days, but has put himself solidly in the service of the new American empire, hoping it will pick up where the British and the French left off.[123]

The average American who sees one such as Bernard Lewis promoted in the broadcast media has no idea that this "kindly old gentleman"—who looks like somebody's grandfather —is, in fact, one of the prime movers behind the most vicious type of racism and religious hatred imaginable, nor will the major media ever reveal that, at least not in America.

THE STRANGE CASE OF JARED TAYLOR

On a far lower level and on assuredly a less widely-publicized scale, certain elements have joined the ranks of the "neo-conservative" elite in promoting anti-Arab and anti-Muslim hatred.

While many Americans of the so-called "extreme right"—not to be confused with the "neo-conservative" movement surrounding Richard Perle and William Kristol and their allies such as Steven Emerson and Bernard Lewis—are strongly anti-Zionist or outright anti-Jewish, there are a handful of other so-called "rightist" organizations that share the anti-Muslim and anti-Arab fanaticism of the Jewish neo-conservatives.

For example, there is one rather prominent individual who—while often described by the media as a "racist"—has nonetheless actively avoided criticizing Israel and who is an outspoken enemy of Arab and Muslim immigrants into America. His name is Jared Taylor.

Editor of a publication known as *American Renaissance*, Jared Taylor is widely believed by many of his critics to be an asset of the CIA.

Critics note not only that he is a graduate of Yale, a long-time CIA recruiting ground, but that he has been active and successful in business and finance in the Far East. In addition, a book Taylor wrote—*Paved With Good Intentions*—alleging that black Americans are inferior to whites, was praised in *Commentary*, the neo-conservative voice of the American Jewish Committee, edited by Norman Podhoretz who, himself, was connected to CIA-financed activities as far back as the 1950s.

So Taylor's connections to the "neo-conservative" network and the New York elite are firm indeed.

And considering the impact that Taylor has in certain American "right wing" circles that are seemingly independent of the "neo-conservative" elite—such as a so-called "Council of Conservative Citizens" of which he is director—it is clear that Taylor's voice is being heard and having an impact. At one juncture, Taylor's Council of Conservative Citizens featured an item attacking "Dirty Rotten Arabs and Muslims" on its website.

The record shows Taylor has a long history of attacking Arabs and Muslims. As far back as November 1993—nearly a decade ago, long before the widespread anti-Muslim tendencies in America, stoked by the major broadcast media, particularly in the wake of the 9-11-2001 terrorist attacks, Taylor's *American Renaissance* magazine featured an article entitled "The Rise of Islam in America," which asserted that "Islam lies at a dangerous intersection between race and immigration," and which declared:

> Islam, in its various forms, lies at the intersection of America's two most dogma-laden and self-destructive policies: immigration and race relations. It was the purest idiocy to have imported crowds of swarthy fanatics who are prepared to kill each other—and us—over obscure conflicts in the Levant. Had no one noticed that Middle Easterners fight out their unsettled feuds not only in their own countries but in Europe as well? To have imported fanatics who worship the same god as the Black Muslims was idiocy on stilts.[124]

A Muslim-bashing hate festival sponsored by Taylor in the Washington, D.C. area over the Feb. 22, 2002 weekend set off alarm bells about Taylor's covert agenda. *American Free Press*, based in Washington, D.C., reported as follows:

> Had you walked into Jared Taylor's recent American Renaissance conference, you might have thought you were at a pro-Israel rally: the anti-Muslim rhetoric was that pervasive. Taylor's self-styled "uptown" approach echoes the ongoing Israeli propaganda theme that the Islamic religion is the root cause of the Sept. 11 tragedy—not the pro-Israel U.S. Middle East policy.
>
> One who attended the meeting—young Bill White—described Taylor's meeting at his (White's) overthrow.com website. While finding the event inter-

esting, White—an outspoken anti-Zionist—says what disturbed him the most was "the decided anti-Black and anti-Muslim tilt of the conference."

The "entire focus," said White, "was on Islam and blacks and how bad and threatening they are, with nary a word about Jews and their influence in politics. All of the speakers either didn't address the Zionist-Israeli issue, or did so in philo-Semitic, flattering, untrue and ridiculous terms." Every speaker at Taylor's conference except one was anti-black and anti-Muslim, according to White.[125]

Perhaps in keeping with his decidedly anti-Muslim stance, Taylor previously featured a hard-line pro-Zionist New York-based Rabbi, Meyer Schiller, as the keynote speaker at a previous conference.

The *Forward* newspaper, a prominent American Jewish publication, has said that Schiller reports that his influence with Taylor has helped bring about positive feelings for the American Jewish cause on Taylor's part, and thereby helped stimulate other Americans who follow Taylor's teachings to think likewise.

Although—after being widely criticized by many of his associates— Taylor has since made some motions to suggest that U.S. policy toward Israel and the Arab world may have stimulated the 9-11 terrorist attacks, Taylor does not relent in his attacks on Muslim immigrants, effectively playing into the hands of the Zionist cause.

Ironically, although Taylor has spent a great deal of energy in Muslim-bashing, his closest friend and long-time political fellow-traveler, one Mark Weber, has assiduously courted the Muslim world while posturing as an "anti-Zionist," causing some persons to wonder just what the Taylor-Weber agenda really may be.

Weber is best known today as one of a small group who—working under the direction of a known long-time CIA operative Andrew E. Allen—orchestrated the destruction of *The Spotlight* newspaper, in its time the one independent American newspaper that regularly and forcefully raised questions about the imbalanced U.S. policy toward Israel and the Arab and Muslim worlds.

Taylor and his ilk are thus part and parcel of a malicious and wide-ranging effort to defame the Arab and Muslim peoples, and the truth is that their impact is being felt at a critical time when the Zionist lobby finds it vital to have its "agents" inside even the smallest—but still mildly influential—groups in America.

Individuals such as these use their outreach (however minimal it may be) to bend Americans and others in the West in favor of Israel through attacks on Arabs and Muslims, and this proves critical to Israel's imperial goals, in league with the neo-conservative manipulators now dominating American foreign policy.

WAS 9-11 THE 'NEW PEARL HARBOR'?

Writing in Britain's *New Statesman* on December 12, 2002, journalist John Pilger described, in disturbing terms, how William Kristol's Project for the New American Century had determined that America needed a "new Pearl Harbor" as the pretext for launching a bid for global dominance. The theme laid forth by Kristol and his associates was that should such a catastrophic event take place, it would give America the opportunity to once again build up its military forces.

On June 3, 1997—three years before George W. Bush assumed the presidency and installed the neo-conservatives in power—a host of neo-conservatives including Donald Rumsfeld, Dick Cheney and Paul Wolfowitz signed their names to a "statement of principles" issued by Kristol's organization.

The statement laid forth a goal of building up American military might to ensure that the United States could pursue global hegemony, unfettered by any nation or nations that might dare to resist the agenda of America's ruling elite—unquestionably a declaration of imperial aims.

A subsequent design—dated September 2000—by Kristol's Project for the New American Century, entitled "Rebuilding America's Defenses: Strategies, Forces and Resources for a New Century," laid forth a plan for the United States to take military control of the Gulf region whether Saddam Hussein was in power or not. It stated frankly that the American need for a presence in the Persian (i.e. Arabian) Gulf transcended the question of whether or not Saddam Hussein remained in power.

In order to fulfill that dream, Kristol and his associates said, the United States must be prepared to be able to do battle in multiple places, at one time, around the globe. To achieve that ability, they declared, America must engage in a major transformation of its military, accompanied by massive arms buildups. However, they concluded, "The process of transformation is likely to be a long one, absent some catastrophic and catalyzing event—like a new Pearl Harbor."

Given that the tragic events of September 11, 2001 provided precisely the "new Pearl Harbor" that sparked a massive build-up, accompanied by the "war on terrorism" that transformed—through neo-conservative influence—into an imperial war, first targeting Iraq and thence the rest of the Arab and Muslim world, there are many Americans and others who question whether the 9-11 attacks were either instigated and/or sponsored by the United States and/or the government of Israel, acting either together or alone. Such people are denounced as "conspiracy theorists" and/or as "hatemongers"—facts notwithstanding.

(The special report from *American Free Press* [AFP]—entitled "Fifty Unanswered Questions About 9-11"—contains a wealth of information in this regard that has otherwise, quite notably, gone unmentioned in the mainstream media in America. The work of AFP's international correspondent, Christopher Bollyn, has been frequently cited as among the most forthright in challenging the official U.S. government scenario as to what happened on that tragic day.)

ONE SCENARIO FOR CREATING TERRORISM . . .

Many Americans who suspect such a scenario point out that there is evidence that, in past years, American officials seriously pondered the possibility of carrying out acts of terrorism on American soil. Most frequently cited is the book by respected veteran journalist James Bamford, *Body of Secrets*, released in 2001—just prior to the 9-11 attacks.

In that book Bamford revealed that as early as January of 1961, top U.S. policy makers were considering a horrific scheme to launch terrorist attacks on American citizens and point the finger of blame at Fidel Castro's communist Cuba.

Although Bamford's book received some media play, Bamford's shocking revelations regarding the terror campaign proposed by then-Joint Chiefs of Staff Chairman, Army General Lyman Lemnitzer, were largely suppressed.

Lemnitzer, reportedly Jewish, later emerged as part of the neo-conservative Committee on the Present Danger, the public advocacy group for the policies put forth by Richard Perle's Team B experiment which was described earlier in these pages. In any case, here's what Bamford wrote:

> According to documents obtained for *Body of Secrets*, Lemnitzer and the Joint Chiefs proposed secretly to stage an attack on the American naval base at Guantanamo Bay, Cuba—and then blame the violent action on Castro. Convinced that Cuba had launched an unprovoked attack on the United States, the unwitting American public would then support the Joint Chiefs' bloody Caribbean war. After all, who would believe Castro's denials over the word of the Pentagon's top military commanders? The nation's most senior military leadership was proposed to launch a war, which would no doubt kill many American servicemen, based solely on a fabric of lies. On January 19, just hours before [then-President Dwight] Eisenhower left office, Lemnitzer gave his approval to the proposal. As events progressed, the plan would become only the tip of a very large and secret iceberg.[126]

A self-described "imaginative planner," Lemnitzer kept his initial plan in cold storage. However, after the new Kennedy administration's Bay of Pigs fiasco which left Fidel Castro stronger than ever before, Lemnitzer reinvigorated his scheme under the name "Operation Northwoods." Bamford reports that:

> The plan, which had the written approval of the chairman and every member of the Joint Chiefs of Staff, called for innocent people to be shot on American streets; for boats carrying refugees fleeing Cuba to be sunk on the high seas; for a wave of violent terrorism to be launched in Washington, D.C., Miami and elsewhere. People would be framed for bombings they did not commit; planes would be hijacked. Using phony evidence, all of it would be blamed on Castro, thus giving Lemnitzer and his cabal the excuse, as well as the public and international backing, they needed to launch their war.[127]

What makes this so additionally disturbing is that this was not some wild scheme by "mad bombers" inside the military. In Bamford's estimation, "the idea may actually have originated with President Eisenhower in the last days of his administration."[128]

Bamford reports that Eisenhower was determined to invade Cuba and that if Castro did not provide an excuse prior to the inauguration of newly-elected President John F. Kennedy, Eisenhower suggested that the United States "could think of manufacturing something that would be generally acceptable."[129]

What Eisenhower was suggesting, writes Bamford, was "a bombing, an attack, an act of sabotage carried out secretly against the United States by the United States. Its purpose would be to justify the launching of a war. It was a dangerous suggestion by a desperate president."[130] Lemnitzer, Eisenhower's protege, was eager to carry out the plan.

Lemnitzer also had in mind the possibility of terrorism on American soil by Americans against Americans—but blamed on Castro. This terrorist conspiracy against his fellow Americans was also offered up by Lemnitzer and his advisors who suggested:

> We could develop a Communist Cuban terror campaign in the Miami area, in other Florida cities and even in Washington. The terror campaign could be pointed at Cuban refugees seeking haven in the United States . . . . We could sink a boatload of Cubans en route to Florida (real or simulated) . . . . We could foster attempts on lives of Cuban refugees in the United States even to the extent of wounding in instances to be widely publicized.[131]

Bombings and, notably, even airplane hijackings, were all suggested. Whether Lemnitzer's proposals ever actually reached President Kennedy is unknown, writes Bamford, but it is clear that the president was not enamored with the war-mongering general to whom he denied a second term as chairman of the Joint Chiefs.

Yet, following in Lemnitzer's tradition, like-minded "intellectuals" in the defense establishment continued to formulate plans passed on to the military leadership that were designed to provoke a war through a staged terrorist attack. In the end, however, no such plan ever seems to have gone beyond the planning stages, at least as far as Cuba was concerned.

The question arises as to whether—on September 11, 2001—another uch insidious scheme was carried through to its conclusion. Many Americans will continue to wonder if that is precisely what happened and evidence continues to emerge that suggests that was indeed the case.

A MUCH BIGGER GAME BEING PLAYED?

As far back as 1975, top imperialist policy makers such as Henry Kissinger were viewing a potential Middle East war as the means by which an imperial world hegemon could be set in place.

In fact, the scenario seems to suggest that the whole Arab-Israeli conflict over Palestine was instigated—from the beginning—for the very purpose of sparking a global war.

This eye-opening scenario was presented in the stunning final (and probably little-read) paragraphs of a now long-forgotten 1975 book, *The Arabs: Their History, Aims and Challenge to the Industrialized World* by American pro-Zionist writer, Thomas Kiernan.

Although Kiernan did not name the top policy maker who outlined this amazing geopolitical scheme, Kiernan did describe the individual asserting this worldview as "a senior American State Department official who has played a central role in the mediatory efforts of Henry Kissinger during the past two years."

This description, of course, could include Kissinger himself and, if truth be told, the speaker was probably Kissinger. If not, the speaker certainly reflected Kissinger's thinking as a key player in Kissinger's global machinations.

Responding to a question by Kiernan as to whether the Middle East conflict could be resolved without world war, the speaker (perhaps Kissinger) asserted:

> The evolution of events in the Middle East during this century can be likened to the construction, if you can imagine it, of an inverted pyramid.
>
> The capstone, which in the case of such a pyramid turns out to be its base, was formed out of the inevitable conflict between foreign Zionists' need and ambition on the one hand, and local Arab pride and aspiration on the other.[132]

Note that the speaker admits that the conflict resulting from the insertion of the Zionist state into Arab territory in Palestine was "inevitable." There have been those who have said, for a generation, that this was the whole purpose of the provocative establishment of Israel in the first place. The speaker continued:

> As the pyramid grew, the stones in each of its successively widening tiers had added to them further elements—the passions and needs of other foreign interests, the passions and aspirations of other national groups within the Arab world. Each succeeding tier sucked more of the world into it. Now the pyramid is finished. And there it stands, incongruously balanced on its point, its four sides reaching up and out into every corner of the world.[133]

In other words, the crisis in the Middle East began drawing in the rest of the nations of the world—similar, precisely, to what is now happening with the ongoing struggle today between the United States and traditional allies such as France and Germany, not to mention the opposition of Russia and China, over the issue of war with Iraq—an outgrowth of the Israel-Palestine conflict itself. The scenario painted continues:

> We all know that it is impossible for a pyramid to stand freely in such an upside-down manner. So far, it has been supported on its four corners by the rest of the world.
>
> Although it has precariously tipped now and then, it has managed to remain more or less upright. But the effort to keep it upright has imposed greater and greater tension on those who support it.
>
> Tension is resolved in two ways, our psychologists tell us. One way is through outburst. The other is through withdrawal. The fight-or-flee mechanism which is part of every human being's reaction system.
>
> Now, you tell me. Will it be resolved peacefully? Or will it take a world war to bring about a resolution?
>
> If my analogy is correct, there can be no question of the ultimate outcome.[134]

In other words, a world war must result as a consequence of the Israeli-Arab conflict. The scenario proceeds:

> One way or the other—whether one side or the other relaxes its support of the pyramid and withdraws, or whether one side or the other chooses to eradicate its tension through outburst—the pyramid will lose its balance and come tumbling down.
>
> Either way, the resolution of the situation will come out of the dust and rubble of the collapsed pyramid. The Israeli-Arab conflict, the very thing that started it all, will be forgotten.[135]

Again, note the suggestion that the Israeli-Arab conflict is indeed central to the world war described in this frightening outline. The scenario concluded:

> East and West will be left to pick over the remains like buzzards dining on carrion. That is, if there still is an East and West.[136]

Note the closing words: "if there still is an East and West." What nations will be allied as "the East" and which as "the West"?

Are new alignments emerging—taking the place of the traditional Cold War era of "USA vs. USSR"?

Is the Arab world—along with the rest of mankind—simply a pawn in a much larger game in which the neo-conservatives are only tools themselves?

The final outcome of the drive for a world empire—dictated by American military might in the hands of a select few, a clique of hard-line neo-conservative war-hawks, the "high priests of war"—remains to be seen. However, based on what we have witnessed thus far, much blood has been shed and will continue to flow.

America's disastrous venture in Iraq is just the beginning—**and** just beginning. Since George W. Bush first declared "victory" in Iraq, things have only gotten worse. America's short-lived triumph has been turning into a Vietnam-style debacle—and the bodybags continue coming home.

The neo-conservative myth about Saddam's "weapons of mass destruction" has long ago been declared the lie that well-informed people knew it was. Many grass-roots Americans are now coming to realize that the pretext for the war against Iraq was nothing more than old-fashioned lies and propaganda, pure and simple.

The truth is: the President of the United States lied to the American people and to the entire world. He was influenced in so doing by his neo-conservative advisors—liars all—and they have effectively set the stage for the deaths of more and more Americans and people worldwide. A world-wide conflagration could indeed be the final result.

There is absolutely nothing "American" or "patriotic" about the ideological or religious or geo-political motivations of the neo-conservative High Priests of War, although today they claim to be the real patriots, the real leaders, the real fighters for American traditions. Nothing could be further from the truth.

America—and the world—will be best served by a forthright and unswerving drive to exorcise these predators once and for all.

The time has indeed come. **Something** has to be done.

A FINAL WORD . . .

**Who will be ruling America . . .
when America is ruling the New World Order?**

**An examination of "the secret agenda behind the agenda"
of the High Priests of War.**

The United Nations—as we have known it—can effectively be considered a ghost of the past. The UN has been shelved, sidelined, consigned to the trash heap—at least temporarily—by the one world dreamers who once saw the global body as the means of establishing a world hegemon. Today's imperialists now envision Uncle Sam as their officially-designated world policeman or, in their more academic terms "the center of a new international system."[137] The goal is "a world that looks like America, and is therefore safe for all."

However, despite the rhetoric—which might please the ears of many grass-roots American patriots (or those who fancy themselves that)—it's not quite so simple. There's more to this agenda than meets the eye.

What might be described as The Grand Scheme for a New World Order—in the wake of America's new "imperial" role—was imparted in quite candid fashion in a major two-part policy paper in the Summer 2003 and Winter 2004 issues of *The Journal of International Security Affairs*, house organ of the definitively influential Jewish Institute for National Security Policy (JINSA), which has been referenced repeatedly in the pages of *The High Priests of War*.

Once a previously little-known Washington think tank, JINSA is now often publicly acknowledged as perhaps the most specific guiding force behind Bush administration foreign policy today. So when something appears in a JINSA publication, there's a lot of weight behind it.

The author, Alexander H. Joffe, a pro-Israel academic, has been a featured writer in the pages of this JINSA publication, and that he was given so much space to tout his theories certainly reflects the high regard in which his views are held.

Joffe's two-part series was entitled "The Empire That Dared Not

Speak Its Name." In his essay, Joffee frankly admitted that "America is an empire" and asserts that, yes, this is a very good thing.

Joffe says that when the UN dared to take on Zionism, that marked the demise of the UN in the minds of the internationalists. Joffe writes: "The end of the General Assembly as a credible body may plausibly be ascribed to the infamous 'Zionism is Racism' resolution in 1975." The JINSA author contends that the world should be "grateful" that the UN has been "discredited, reduced to farce and ultimately ground to a halt," referring, of course, to UN positions that the Zionists and their allies in the world empire movement find offensive.

As a result of the UN being shelved as a world government vehicle, writes Joffe, "We now have the opportunity, and obligation, to begin again." However, he warns that the emerging European Union (EU) is a threat to the dream of a global empire.

The JINSA writer asserts that the EU is an "alternative vision for the international community," one that, as he puts it, frankly is "the authentic countervision to an American Empire." According to the Zionist writer, the biggest problem with Europe and the EU is that "culture remains at the core of Europe's problems. Nationalism was a doctrine born in Europe, as were its vicious mutant offspring: fascism and communism."

(Note: A fervent advocate of Israeli super-nationalism, the writer, Joffe, doesn't seem to see the lack of logic in his attack on *other* peoples' nationalism—but then, again, honesty has never been integral to the hardline Zionist point of view.)

Joffe complains that although "the new European Empire is multicultural in theory . . . in reality it is dominated politically and culturally by France and economically by Germany." Today, in the EU, he says, "driven by a sense of postcolonial guilt and postwar ennui the door have been thrown open to all ideas. At the most sinister levels it has permitted and even legitimized a vast explosion of unhinged thought and action, namely anti-Americanism, anti-Semitism, and a wide variety of conspiracy theories."

(The so-called "conspiracy theories" that so alarm this Zionist theoretician are those that dare to challenge the "official" views of what really happened on September 11, 2001. He is inflamed that millions of people in Europe and the Muslim world—not to mention the United States—

have raised questions about Israeli foreknowledge and/or involvement in those events.)

In any case, what Joffe describes as "the other kind of liberal internationalism" is what the Zionist movement favors and Joffe defines it:

> The American Empire has no real or theoretical competitors. The goal of the American Empire in the 21st century is not territorial control or the exploitation of resources but political and economic leadership which defends and advances American interests, and which promotes the development and well being of all nations. Given our history and our values, that future lies in leveraging the American Empire in such a way that it becomes the basis of a new democratic international system.
>
> Ultimately the only answer for a stable and prosperous planet will be a global system that is structurally and morally similar to the American union—semi-autonomous states with secular, liberal democratic systems; where states have both prescribed rights and agreed upon responsibilities in a larger secular, liberal democratic framework; one equipped with checks and balances and meaningful institutions; with governance based on rule of law and tolerant and pluralist values.

In the second-part of his extended essay, published in the Winter 2004 issue of JINSA's journal, Joffe pursued this line of thought further, expanding on his call for what he described as "an empire that looks like America."[138]

Amazingly, Joffe frankly talks about the United States engaging in massive imperial conquests in the trouble-torn regions of Africa—presumably after the United States has already made havoc in the Arab countries of the Middle East:

> The conditions under which America and its allies would simply take over and restore African countries are far from clear. What are the thresholds for intervention? What are the procedures and outcomes? Who will fight and who will pay? The restoration of Africa would involve long-term commitments and immense costs, of the sort that could only be paid for by Africa itself. That is to say, it would probably require American economic control, to go along with political and cultural control. Colonialism is always pay as you go, and it is not pretty. The question is both whether Africa can pay the price (or afford not to) and whether America has the stomach.

Of course, Africa is not the only target of Joffe and his like-minded schemers (and that is precisely what they are, however, "extreme" that term may be perceived). In fact, Joffe talks of a wide-ranging global agenda—well beyond the African continent.

In the end, however, Joffe lets the cat out of the bag, about the real intentions of those who are using United States military power as the mechanism for a bigger agenda. "New arrangements," he says, "must come into being under American leadership to provide an alternative for states that are willing to accept rights and responsibilities." Joffe dreams of a United Nations that has been re-made under the imperial force of the United States. And ultimately, he predicts the possibility of a world government, writing:

> Possibly, after a period of chaos and anger, which in any event would simply intensify existing states of being, the institution [the United Nations] might be bludgeoned into changing. [Note his use of the term "bludgeoned."—MCP]
>
> Rather than a club that admits all, the 21st century United Nations might—someday, somehow—be remade into an exclusive, by invitation, members-only group, of free, democratic states, sharing similar values. Or in the end, replaced by one. That day, however, may be decades off.

Should there be any doubt that he is talking about world government, note Joffe's concluding words:

> The best way to preserve the American empire is to eventually give it up. Setting the stage for global governance can only be done with American leadership and American-led institutions of the sort schematically outlined here.

So it is. Despite all the high-sounding rhetoric about "democracy," what it all comes down to—in the words of this pro-Israel ideologue—is the use of America's military power to advance another (secret) agenda altogether. Even many of those grass-roots American flag-wavers (who may be genuine patriots) who relish the concept of an American empire may find Joffe's concepts somewhat different from what they otherwise might perceive.

But here, in the pages of a devotedly pro-Zionist journal, we learn precisely what the "story behind the story" actually happens to be. It has nothing to do, really, even with a "strong America" or, for that matter, even with America itself.

The United States of America is simply a pawn—albeit a powerful one—in the game, being ruthlessly shifted about in a scheme for world dominance by an elite few operating behind the scenes.

And, in the end, this does tell us very much about who The High Priests of War really are and what their agenda is really all about. There's no mystery at all.

What remains to be determined is what the American people—and all other real patriots in nations around the globe—intend to do about it.

The question is this: will the world finally decide it *is* time to declare war on The High Priests of War?

—MICHAEL COLLINS PIPER

Endnotes

[1] Reported in multiple media sources including *The New York Times* on March 15, 2003.

[2] *Forward*, Feb. 28, 2003. (Kinsey's cited comments appeared online at *Slate* magazine at slate.com in an article dated Oct. 24, 2002.)

[3] *Ibid.*

[4] *Ha'aretz*, April 9, 2003.

[5] Philip S. Golub. "Inventing Demons." *Counterpunch* magazine online at counterpunchorg, April 5, 2003. English-language translation republished from *LeMonde Diplomatique*.

[6] Michael Lind. *Made in Texas: George W. Bush and the Southern Takeover of American Politics*. (New York: Basic Books, 2003), p. 138.

[7] Stanley Heller writing on Feb. 20, 2003 at antiwar.com

[8] Professor Paul Gottfried, March 20, 2003 at http://www.lewrockwell.com/gottfried/gottfried47.html.

[9] *The Sacramento Union*, June 29, 1986.

[10] Jonathan Clarke. *The National Interest*. Spring 2001.

[11] Michael Lind. *Made in Texas: George W. Bush and the Southern Takeover of American Politics*. (New York: Basic Books, 2003), p. 132.

[12] "Distorting US Foreign Policy: The Israel Lobby and American Power." Michael Lind. *Prospect*, April 2002.

[13] *Ibid.*

[14] "Group Urges Pro-Israel Leaders' Silence on Iraq." *Washington Post*, Nov. 27, 2002.

[15] Michael Lind. *Made in Texas: George W. Bush and the Southern Takeover of American Politics*. (New York: Basic Books, 2003), pp. 140-141.

[16] *Time*, February 17, 2003.

[17] *Ha'aretz*, February 18, 2003.

[18] *Ibid.*

[19] James Bennett writing in *The New York Times*, Feb. 27, 2003.

[20] See ADL website at adl.org. Statement issued dated March 21, 2003.

[21] "The Bloodstained Path," Dennis Kucinich. *The Progressive*, November 2002.

[22] Statement by Congressman Kucinich found at: http://www.kucinich.us/

[23] US *Congressional Record*. Senate proceedings. March 19, 2003.

[24] Bill and Kathleen Christison, writing in *Counterpunch* magazine at counterpunch.org, Dec. 13, 2002.

[25] Cited by Christison, *Ibid.*

[26] *Ibid.*

[27] *Wall Street Journal*, March 21, 2003.

[28] *New York Times*, March 24, 2003.

[29] *Forward*, March 21, 2003.

[30] *Ibid.*

[31] *Ibid.*

[32] Michael Lind. *Made in Texas: George W. Bush and the Southern Takeover of American Politics*. (New York: Basic Books, 2003), p. 138.

[33] Benjamin Ginsberg. *The Fatal Embrace: Jews and The State*. (Chicago: University of Chicago Press), 1993., pp. 204-205.

[34] *The Nation*, March 22, 1986.

[35] *The Neo-Conservatives: The Men Who Are Changing America's Politics*. (New York: Simon & Schuster, 1979), p. 1.

36 Ibid., p. 81.

37 Frances Stonor Saunders. *The Cultural Cold War*. (New York: The New Press, 1999).

38 Sidney Blumenthal. *The Rise of the Counter-Establishment: From Conservative Ideology to Political Power*. (New York: Times Books, 1986), p. 148.

39 Ibid., p. 159.

40 Sidney Blumenthal, p. 154.

41 *The Washington Post*, March 19, 2002.

42 *Ibid.*

43 Eric Alterman. *The Nation*, Dec. 23, 1986.

44 Stephen D. Isaacs. *Jews and American Politics*. (New York: Doubleday & Company, 1975), p. 254.

45 Anne Hessing Cahn, *Bulletin of Atomic Scientists*. April 1993. Online at thebulletin.org/issues/1993/a93/a93Teamb.html.

46 Anne Hessing Cahn. *Killing Détente: The Right Attacks the CIA* (State College, Pennsylvania: Pennsylvania State University Press, 1998), p. 151.

47 *Ibid*. p. 30.

48 *Ibid.*, p. 187.

49 *The Spotlight*, Feb. 5, 1996.

50 *Ibid.*

51 John Ehrman. *The Rise of Neo-Conservatism: Intellectuals and Foreign Affairs*, (New Haven, Connecticut: University of Connecticut Press), 1995., p. 112.

52 Ginsberg, p. 205.

53 Ginsberg, p. 205.

54 Richard Gid Powers. *Not Without Honor: The History of American Anti-Communism*. (New York: Free Press), 1995, p. 393.

55 *New York Times*, Nov. 23, 1981.

56 John Ehrman, pp. 139-141.

57 Anne Hessing Cahn in *Bulletin of Atomic Scientists*. April 1993. Online at thebulletin.org/issues/1993/a93/a93Teamb.html.

58 *Ibid.*

59 The Bryen affair is documented in detail in *The Armageddon Network*, by Michael Saba. (Brattleboro, Vermont: Amana Books, 1977)

60 *Business Week*, May 21, 1984.

61 *The Washington Post Magazine*, April 13, 1986.

62 "U.S. Secrets and the Israelis." *Boston Globe* editorial. August 28, 1986.

63 *New York Times*, May 3, 1986.

64 All quoted remarks from: *Wall Street Journal*, Jan. 22, 1992.

65 *Ibid.*

66 *The Weekly Standard*, March 17, 2003.

67 "Bill Kristol, Keeping Iraq in the Cross Hairs," *Washington Post*. March 18, 2003.

68 *Washington Post*, Aug. 21, 2001.

69 All quotations: *Ibid.*

70 Michael Lind. *Made in Texas: George W. Bush and the Southern Takeover of American Politics*. (New York: Basic Books, 2003), p. 131.

71 *The Boston Globe*, March 23, 2003.

72 "Bush's Grand Strategy," Andrew J. Bacevich, *American Conservative*, Nov. 4, 2002.

73 "America's Age of Empire," Todd Gitlin. *Mother Jones*, Jan/Feb. 2003.

74 Gitlin, *Ibid.*

75 "In Praise of the Bush Doctrine," Norman Podhoretz, *Commentary*, Sept. 2002.

76 *Ibid.*

[77] *Ibid.*

[78] *The Washington Post*, August 1, 2002.

[79] *The Washington Post*, July 28, 2002.

[80] *Ibid.*

[81] *Washington Monthly*, June 2002.

[82] *Ibid.*

[83] *Ibid.*

[84] *The Washington Post*, Oct. 16, 2002

[85] All quotes, *Ibid.*

[86] *Ibid.*

[87] Michael Lind. *Made in Texas: George W. Bush and the Southern Takeover of American Politics*. (New York: Basic Books, 2003), pp. 133-134.

[88] time.com, Feb. 5, 2003.

[89] *New York Review of Books*, February 13, 2003

[90] *Ibid.*

[91] *Washington Post*, Jan. 13, 2003.

[92] *The Washington Post*, Feb. 9, 2003.

[93] *Washington Times*, Feb. 14, 2003.

[94] Michael Ledeen. *The War Against the Terror Masters*. (New York: Truman Talley Books/St. Martin's Press, 2002), pp. 212-213.

[95] *Ibid.*, p.236.

[96] *The Washington Post*, Oct. 30, 1993.

[97] *The New Yorker*, April 7, 2003.

[98] Michael Lind. *Made in Texas: George W. Bush and the Southern Takeover of American Politics*. (New York: Basic Books, 2003), p. 157.

[99] *The New Republic*, Jan. 29, 2001.

[100] Kathleen & Bill Christison in *Counterpunch* magazine at counterpunch.org, Dec. 13, 2002

[101] Benjamin Ginsberg. *The Fatal Embrace: Jews and The State*. (Chicago: University of Chicago Press), 1993, p. 211.

[102] Lind, p. 149.

[103] "Born Again Zionists," Ken Silverstein and Michael Scherer, *Mother Jones*, Sept./Oct. 2002.

[104] *Ibid.*

[105] Silverstein & Scherer, *Mother Jones. Ibid.*

[106] *Ibid.*

[107] Lind, p. 148.

[108] *Ibid.*

[109] *Ibid.*

[110] *Congressional Record*, Senate. March 4, 2002.

[111] Cited in Michael Lind. *Made in Texas: George W. Bush and the Southern Takeover of American Politics*. (New York: Basic Books, 2003), p. 153.

[112] *The Washington Times*, Jan. 22, 2003.

[113] *The Washington Times*, Aug. 13, 2001.

[114] *Ibid.*

[115] Until otherwise noted, all quotations which follow are excerpted from: Edward Herman and Gerry O'Sullivan. *The 'Terrorism' Industry: The Experts and Institutions That Shape Our View of Terror*. (New York: Pantheon Books, 1989).

[116] John F. Sugg, *Fair EXTRA*, January/February 1999 at www.fair.org/extra/9901/emerson.html

[117] Anis Shivani, writing in *Counterpunch* magazine at counterpunch.org, Sept. 14-15, 2002.

[118] *Ibid.*

119 *Ibid.*

120 *New York Times*, April 5, 2003.

121 Cited by Lamis Andoni, writing in "Bernard Lewis: In the Service of Empire" published online at *The Electronic Intifada*, Dec. 16, 2002 (see electronicIntifada.net).

122 *Ibid.*

123 *Ibid.*

124 *American Renaissance*, Nov. 1993.

125 *American Free Press*, March 11, 2002.

126 James Bamford, *Body of Secrets*. (New York: Doubleday, 2001), p. 71.

127 *Ibid.*, p. 82.

128 *Ibid.*

129 *Ibid.*, p. 83.

130 *Ibid.*

131 *Ibid.*, pp. 84-85.

132 Thomas Kiernan. *The Arabs.* (Boston: Little Brown & Company, 1975), p. 425.

133 *Ibid.*

134 *Ibid.*, p. 426.

135 *Ibid.*

136 *Ibid.*

137 Until otherwise noted, the cited quotations which follow are taken from the Summer 2003 *Journal of International Security Affairs*, published by the Jewish Institute for National Security Affairs in Washington, D.C. See their website at JINSA.org.

138 Until otherwise noted, the cited quotations which follow are taken from the Winter 2004 *Journal of International Security Affairs*, published by the Jewish Institute for National Security Affairs in Washington, D.C. See their website at JINSA.org.

GRAND ETAT D'ISRAEL
DU NIL JUSQU' À L'EUPHRATE

GREATER ISRAEL
FROM THE NILE TO THE EUPHRATES

This map illustrates what the hard-line American neo-conservatives and their allies in Israel perceive to be the ultimate bound-
aries of what is known as "Greater Israel." Although the neo-conservatives deny this is their goal, the truth is that numerous
Zionist leaders, over the years, have frankly outlined the dream
of "Greater Israel." Note that the borders of Greater Israel incor-
porate quite a bit of territory that the non-Jewish people of the
world recognize as belonging to other countries. In fact, most people (even many well-informed intellectuals) have no idea this concept of "Greater Israel" is integral to the neo-conservative point
of view and that the American war against Iraq was a first step in
the drive toward the goal of achieving "Greater Israel." The policies of the neo-conservative clique that controls the administration of American President George W.
Bush (bottom left) are aligned ideologically and geopolitically with Israel's hard-line
Likud expansionists allied with Israel's Ariel "The Butcher" Sharon (top right).

The resources of media baron Rupert Murdoch (left) are a primary force behind the pro-Israel neo-conservative propaganda network. His publications such as *The New York Post* and *The Weekly Standard* are major voices for Israel's interests. Murdoch's critics contend he is essentially a highly-paid "front man" for billionaire patrons of Israel as Edgar Bronfman, Sr. (center), longtime chief of the World Jewish Congress, and Lord Jacob Rothschild (right) of the legendary European banking empire. Murdoch's propaganda is supplemented by other pro-Israel publishers such as Mortimer Zuckerman (bottom left) who has been chairman of the Conference of Presidents of Major American Jewish Organizations and who owns *U.S. News & World Report*, *The Atlantic*, and *The New York Daily News*, Martin Peretz (bottom center) publisher of the influential *New Republic*, and Korean cult leader Sun Myung Moon (bottom right), a creation of the CIA-controlled Korean intelligence agency. Moon's *Washington Times* newspaper—virtually a Republican house organ—is the "must read" neo-conservative daily in the nation's capital.

William Kristol (left) and his father, Irving Kristol (right) are the leading publicists for the Israeli lobby's neo-conservative network. The younger Kristol—a ubiquitous "talking head" in the media, which gives him endless publicity—acts as publisher/editor of Rupert Murdoch's *Weekly Standard* and operates two major organizations, Empower America and the Project for the New American Century. The elder Kristol—who began as a devoted American follower of Soviet gangster Leon Trotsky (bottom left) and who was later associated with two CIA-funded "cultural" organizations—is the driving force behind two influential journals, *The National Interest* and *The Public Interest* and has been the veritable "godfather" of the neo-conservative movement, even promoting a "war against terrorism" long before the 9-11 terrorist attacks. The Kristols are closely connected to the Lynde and Harry Bradley Foundation which funds many neo-conservative front groups. A longtime Kristol collaborator, going back more than 50 years, is fellow "ex-Trotskyite" Norman Podhoretz (bottom right), whose considerable clout came through his years as editor of *Commentary*, the influential "neo-conservative" journal of the American Jewish Committee. Podhoretz's son, John, initially joined William Kristol at *The Weekly Standard* but is now ensconced at Murdoch's *New York Post* penning pro-Israel screeds.

As far back as the early 1970s, Richard Perle (left) and Frank Gaffney (center) were key operatives for the Israeli lobby on Capitol Hill, working out of the office of then-Senator Henry M. "Scoop" Jackson, a fanatically pro-Israel Democrat from Washington (right) whose presidential ambitions were largely financed by supporters of Israel. While on Jackson's staff, Perle was investigated by the FBI on charges of espionage on behalf of Israel, although the investigation was quashed. Today Perle and Gaffney are key figures in the neo-conservative pro-Israel propaganda network. Other longtime close associates of Perle include former Reagan administration National Security Council staffer Michael Ledeen (bottom left), who actually called for the "creative destruction" of the Arab world, Elliott Abrams (bottom center), the son in law of Norman Podhoretz ("ex-Trotskyite" associate of neo-conservative godfather Irving Kristol) and former Navy Secretary John Lehman (bottom right), who once joined Perle in a venture promoting the interests of an Israeli weapons manufacturer. Abrams is now the Middle East specialist on the George W. Bush administration's National Security Council. Lehman is a member of the commission ostensibly "investigating" the 9-11 terrorist attacks.

During the closing days of the Gerald Ford administration (1974-1976), Richard Perle was a key figure in official Washington organizing and promoting the "Team B" of pro-Israel hard-liners working to advance Israel's cause in the U.S. military and intelligence community. One longtime CIA official who strenuously objected to—and worked behind the scenes to combat—Team B's pro-Israel propagandizing, John Paisley (left) was murdered, almost certainly by Israel's Mossad. Notable among the "hawks" Perle recruited to "Team B" was Paul Wolfowitz (center), who, today—as Deputy Defense Secretary—is the most influential maker of foreign policy in the "Dubya" Bush administration. Wolfowitz and his deputy, Douglas Feith (right), another veteran advocate for Israel, are the real powers behind Defense Secretary Donald Rumsfeld (bottom left). A Wolfowitz protégé, I. Lewis "Scooter" Libby (bottom center), runs the office of Vice President Dick Cheney (bottom right). Prior to the vice presidency, Cheney demonstrated his devotion to Israel by serving on the board of the Perle-connected Jewish Institute for National Security Affairs.

Shown sharing a toast (above) are businessman Michael Saba (left) and the veteran journalist to whom this book is dedicated, Andrew St. George (right). The two worked closely
together for years seeking to publicize the Israeli espionage scandal involving Richard
Perle's longtime associate Stephen J. Bryen (far right). Saba wrote a book about the Bryen
affair, *The Road to Armageddon*, while his friend St. George wrote extensively about the
scandal in the pages of *The Spotlight*, one of the few publications to dare to delve into the
matter. Saba, an Arab-American civil rights activist, happened—by pure chance—to be in
a Washington, D.C. coffee shop at the very time Bryen (then a high-ranking congressional
staffer) was passing classified U.S. defense secrets to Israeli operatives. Saba overheard the
intrigue, and recognizing Bryen, reported what happened to the FBI. Although a Jewish-
American federal prosecutor wanted to indict Bryen for espionage, pressure from Bryen's
highly-placed allies resulted in the indictment being quashed. Bryen was later rewarded
with a top post in the Reagan administration Defense Department as deputy to Richard
Perle and later founded the influential Jewish Institute for National Security Affairs which
is today seen as the guiding force behind the Bush administration's foreign policy.

No account of the lunacy and fanaticism rampant
within neo-conservative circles would be complete without reference to one of Israel's most
devoted advocates in Washington, Attorney
General John Ashcroft (right), shown before the
classic statue—"The Spirit of Justice"—at the
Department of Justice. This photo was taken
before Ashcroft spent $8,000 in taxpayers' money
to cover up the bosom of this fabulous work of
classic art because it offended his sensibilities.
Ashcroft is said to be frightened of calico cats
(inset) because, for religious reasons, he considers
them "tools of the devil." Evidence of peculiar
activity by known Israeli intelligence operatives
on American soil— before and on the day of the
9-11 attacks—has been dismissed by Ashcroft as
an "urban legend." It is not.

A senior player in Richard Perle's power network is aging "Team B" veteran Paul Nitze (left), who, in the early 1960s, was involved in the recently exposed "Operation Northwoods" scheme by another pro-Israel stalwart, General Lyman Lemnitzer (center), to stage terrorist attacks on American soil to be falsely blamed on Cuban dictator Fidel Castro. A younger Perle protege is Daniel Pipes (right), the son of Perle's Team B recruit Richard Pipes. Virulently anti-Arab and anti-Muslim, Pipes has always received vast and friendly media publicity. George W. Bush rewarded Pipes for his hate-mongering with an appointment to the U.S. Institute of Peace which, considering Pipe's presence, is clearly misnamed.

Christopher Bollyn (above) was one of the first journalists to reveal that key neo-conservatives had actually proclaimed a "new Pearl Harbor" could provide a pretext for the U.S to launch a drive for a global imperium. This indeed became the case when "Dubya" Bush launched war against Iraq, having deceived many Americans, through outright lies, that Iraq had played a part in the 9-11 terrorist attacks. Actually, as far back as 1975, infamous intriguer Henry Kissinger (left) was suggesting a Middle East war could provide the foundation for establishing a realigned world of the type of which the neo-conservatives dream.

Three characters who promote Israel's agenda within the so-called "Christian Right" all owe their careers to the patronage of neo-conservative kingpins William and Irving Kristol. William Bennett (left)—named Ronald Reagan's Education Secretary with Irving Kristol's support—gave young Kristol his first high-level government job. Since then Bennett has become a highly-paid author and lecturer and is a co-chair of Kristol's Empower America operation. Former Ambassador Alan Keyes (center), young Kristol's college roommate, made lots of money seeking various offices, paying himself big salaries out of his campaign funds. Gary Bauer (right)—who shares a vacation condominium with Kristol—declares support for Israel central to Christian "family values." Critics contend the "no-chance" candidacies of Keyes and Bauer in the 2000 GOP presidential primaries were instigated by William Kristol who hoped their efforts would draw votes away from Pat Buchanan—a critic of Israel—who was popular among Christian voters because of his opposition to abortion. Significantly more influential on the Christian Right are televangelists (bottom, left to right) Jerry Falwell, Pat Robertson, and Tim LaHaye. The trio has reaped immense profits in broadcasting and publishing deals made possible only because they have been "approved" by powerful pro-Israel families and interests who have an immense, undeniable influence in the media.

When those who control the media agenda want a "scholarly" face to promote attacks on the Arab and Muslim worlds, they turn to Bernard Lewis (left), a British native of the Jewish faith, who is dubbed an authority on the Islamic world, but whose own ethnic antecedents are never mentioned. Lewis—who drapes his bigotry in elegant prose—is the father of a top figure in AIPAC, the lobby for Israel. When the media wants sensational stories of Arab conspiracies, they hype the theories of so-called "terrorism expert" Steven Emerson (center) who is not an "expert," but simply a well-paid hack writer funded by multiple pro-Israel sources. A particularly shrill neo-conservative hate-peddler, Charles Krauthammer (right)—a psychiatrist-turned-pundit who has called for an all-out U.S. war against the Muslim world—surpasses even neo-conservative stalwart George Will in his obsessive interest in endless jabbering about how wonderful Israel is and how awful anyone who criticizes Israel is.

Two close friends, former GOP members of Congress, Newt Gingrich (left) and Vin Weber (right) are reliable voices for the neo-conservative agenda. Gingrich's wife even received a stipend from an Israeli firm while Newt was in Congress. When nailed in the House check-kiting scandal and forced out of office, Weber's courtship of Israel paid off: William Kristol drafted Weber to co-chair his Empower America unit. Weber and Gingrich have also been recruited to the Council on Foreign Relations, "American cousin" to the Rothschild-funded Royal Institute for International Affairs in London.

Senators John McCain (R-Ariz)—left—and Joe Lieberman (D-Conn.)—center—were among the most strident congressional advocates of war against Iraq. Another pro-Israel fanatic, Sen. James Inhofe (right), an Oklahoma Republican, actually claimed on the Senate floor that God opened a spiritual door that allowed the 9-11 attack on the United States because the United States had not been sufficiently supportive of Israel. In contrast, Rep. Jim Moran, a liberal Democrat from Virginia (bottom left), was subjected to national media abuse for suggesting the American Jewish community had enough clout to stop the push for war against Iraq. The media reported—only once and in passing—that Moran's remarks were in response to a friendly question from one of Moran's Jewish constituents who agreed with Moran's opposition to the war. West Virginia's Sen. Robert Byrd (bottom center) and Ohio's Rep. Dennis Kucinich (bottom right) were among the most eloquent and outspoken members of Congress fighting the schemes of the neo-conservatives to bring America into war. The pro-Israel owners of the major broadcast networks and newspapers paid back Kucinich by imposing a virtual blackout on his 2004 presidential campaign.

Although President George W. Bush (left) frequently described Iraqi leader Saddam Hussein (center) as "the guy who tried to kill my dad," referring to a flimsy and apparently baseless conspiracy theory alleging a "plot" by Saddam against former President George H. W. Bush (right), what the younger Bush never mentions is that his father's friend and fellow Republican, former Illinois Rep. Paul Findley (bottom left) revealed in 1992 that former Israeli intelligence officer Victor Ostrovsky (bottom center) had exposed a 1991 plot by a right-wing faction in Israel's Mossad to kill the elder Bush, who they perceived as a threat to Israel. Ostrovsky provided the details to former Rep. Pete McCloskey (bottom right), another Bush friend, who then conveyed a warning about the plot to the Secret Service. In his 1994 book, *The Other Side of Deception*, Ostrovsky reported the Mossad planned to assassinate Bush during a conference in Madrid. Having captured three Palestinian "extremists," the Mossad leaked word to the Spanish police that terrorists were on their way to Madrid. The plan was to kill Bush, release the Palestinians on the scene and kill them on the spot. Bush's assassination would be blamed on the Palestinians—another Mossad "false flag." The major media has never once reported this shocking story.

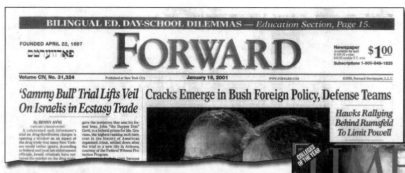

In January of 2001, while grassroots Republicans were celebrating the new Bush administration and cheering greatly admired Gen. Colin Powell—the military hero newly-appointed as secretary of state—readers of Jewish newspapers such as *Forward* were being given a very negative picture of Powell. In a front-page headline story on Jan. 19, 2001 (above), *Forward* announced the Israeli lobby was leery of Powell and that the "hawks"—the neo-conservatives—were maneuvering "to limit his power over foreign policy and boost that of [Defense Secretary] Donald Rumsfeld." As the neo-conservatives began banging the drum for war against Iraq, media voices such as World Jewish Congress chief Edgar Bronfman's *Time* (inset) and then *Newsweek* and its sister publication, *The Washington Post*, followed *Forward*'s lead and began questioning Powell's capabilities. Essentially, Powell's crime was being insufficiently supportive of the demands by the neo-conservatives—most of whom never served in the military—that Americans be sent as cannon fodder for Israel in a war against Iraq. Among the most strident pro-war advocates of "American" imperialism have been (bottom, left to right) *Commentary*, published by the New York chapter of the American Jewish Committee, Rupert Murdoch's *Weekly Standard* (edited by William Kristol) and *U.S. News & World Report*, owned by Mort Zuckerman, chairman of the Conference of Presidents of Major American Jewish Organizations.

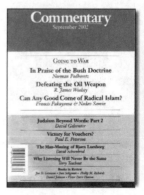

Israel lobby behind Iraq war plan

Khaleeq Times 3/12

By Syed Qamar Hasan

ABU DHABI — Prominent American journalist Michael Collins Piper has said that there is sufficient evidence to confirm the fact that the Israeli lobby was the major force driving Americans to war against Iraq.

Speaking at the Zayed Centre for Coordination and Follow-Up in Abu Dhabi, Mr Piper warned the international community that the Israelis would take advantage of the war and would possibly deport Palestinians, in pursuance of their policy to create 'Greater Israel'.

Author of the acclaimed book, *Final Judgement*, which

MICHAEL COLLINS PIPER

assassination of John F. Kennedy, Mr Piper denounced what he described as the policy of double standards being followed by the US government in dealing with the Iraqi issue.

He called upon the international community to take ser-

inflicted upon the Palestinians by Israel. He said that the Americans were now convinced that any cooperation Saddam Hussein offered to the United Nations in getting rid of weapons of mass destruction would not satisfy President George W. Bush.

Criticising the American bias in favour of Israel, Mr Piper said: "President Bush seems to be driven by Christian fundamentalism and strong influence of the Jewish lobby."

He cited the 1983 Capitol Hill incident when a 22-year old Israeli Jew strapped himself with explosives and threatened to blow up the place.

section," he said.

He also said that the Anti-Defamation League was hand in glove with Mossad and was functioning as an information gathering outfit for the Israeli spy agency.

"Several of the harsh reports in the US media about Saudi Arabia were taken verbatim from a 49- page, *White Paper* issued by the League.

He blamed Israel for the three major crises US polity faced during the latter half of the 20th century. He said the assassination of John. F. Kennedy, the Watergate scandal and the Monica Lewinsky affair had all been consequences of the Israeli policies vis-a

U.S. scribe urges concern for Palestinians

Piper denounounces U.S. double-standards in dealing with issue of mass destruction weapons

By A Staff Reporter

Abu Dhabi

A prominent American journalist has called upon the international community to show more concern to the deprivation, indignity and destruction inflicted upon the Palestinian people.

In a lecture at Zayed Centre for Coordination and Follow-up, Michel Collins Piper, described Israel as a "self-destructive" nation.

On the possibility of deporting the Palestinians outside their homeland, he said this "is likely to be the Israeli policy if American attacks Iraq." This is a part of the Israeli strategy for building Greater Israel, he added.

Piper provided enough evidence to show that the Israeli lobby is

destruction weapons issue. He said the "American citizen is convinced that whatever be the cooperation of Saddam Hussain, it will not satisfy President Bush."

Regarding the notorious book on *Protocols of Zion's Elders*, he said the "Jewish conspiracy is not a mere theory but a real fact."

Piper criticised the American bias towards Israel and suggested that the "President Bush seems to be driven by Christian fundamentalism."

He added that no mention was made on the efforts of Israel to develop a bomb which would eliminate the Arab race.

Piper demonstrated in detail the Zionist influence on the American media through a handful "elite of rich and super rich

Michel Collins Piper

1983, who was found to be an Israeli Jew, 22-year-old Israeli Rabinowits. This story, he added,

close ties with Israel's Mossad and functions as an information gathering outlet for it." Many of the attacks on Saudi Arabia in the major media come practically verbatim from a 49-page 'white paper' issued by the ADL.

Piper went on to Say that the three most talked about and most serious political convulsions that rocked the American system of government during the last half of the 20th century can all be "traced most directly and definitively to the continuing conflict over Palestine and the aggressive imperial role of Israel in Middle East's affairs: they are the assassination of John Kennedy, the Watergate Scandal, and the Monica Lewinsky affair."

Israel and Red China are

In March of 2003—on the eve of the American invasion of Iraq—Michael Collins Piper, the author of *The High Priests of War*, was in Abu Dhabi, the capital of the United Arab Emirates (UAE), as the invited guest of the distinguished Zayed Centre for Coordination and Follow-Up, the official think tank of the League of Arab States. Piper's lecture, on the topic of American media bias in favor of Israel, received highly favorable news coverage in the Arabic and English-language press in the Middle East (see above). However, Piper was shocked to learn that—prodded by the Anti-Defamation League (ADL) of B'nai B'rith—the Bush administration's ambassador to the UAE contacted the Zayed Centre to complain about Piper's lecture, attempting to quash an American citizen's First Amendment rights while he was on foreign soil. The ADL and the Mossad-linked Middle East Media Research Institute (MEMRI) continued to raise such a ruckus about the lectures by Piper and others at the Zayed Centre that the Bush administration finally put so much pressure on the government of Abu Dhabi that the Zayed Centre was shut down, demonstrating that Israeli lobby power even extends, at least indirectly, into the upper reaches of the Arab world.

In 1992 former Rep. Paul Findley remarked that "in all the words written about the assassination of John F. Kennedy, Israel's intelligence agency, the Mossad, has never been mentioned, despite the obvious fact Mossad complicity is as plausible as any of the other theories." However, in 1994, in his book *Final Judgment* (right) Michael Collins Piper—author of *The High Priests of War*—documented the Mossad role's alongside the CIA in the JFK conspiracy. Although never in any major bookstore, some 45,000 copies of *Final Judgment* are now in circulation—more than more widely-publicized books on the topic. Now in its 768-page 6th edition (ordering coupon on page 127) *Final Judgment* explains how JFK's murder set the stage for the Israeli lobby to achieve the immense political power it has today. The book documents that in 1963 JFK (bottom left) was embroiled in a bitter secret conflict with Israeli leader David Ben-Gurion

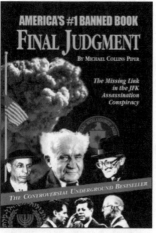

over Israel's drive to build the atomic bomb. Ben-Gurion resigned in disgust, saying that because of JFK, Israel's "existence [was] in danger." Upon JFK's assassination, U.S. policy toward Israel began an immediate 180-degree turnabout. *Final Judgment* documents what Israeli journalist Barry Chamish says is "a pretty cogent case" for Mossad involvement in JFK's murder. The fact is that when New Orleans District Attorney Jim Garrison prosecuted trade executive Clay Shaw with conspiracy in the assassination, Garrison had stumbled on the Mossad link: Shaw served on the board of Permindex, a front for Mossad arms procurement operations. A key Permindex shareholder, the Swiss-based Banque De Credit Internationale, was the fiefdom of Tibor Rosenbaum, a top Mossad official, and chief money laundry for Meyer Lansky, "chairman" of the crime syndicate and Israeli loyalist. The CEO of Permindex was Louis Bloomfield of Montreal, an operative of the Bronfman family, intimate Lansky associates and leading patrons of Israel. *Final Judgment* points out that James Angleton, the CIA's Mossad liaison, was a devoted partisan of Israel who orchestrated a false scenario linking accused assassin Lee Oswald to the Soviet KGB. Even "mainstream" organized crime sources note that leading "Mafia" figures accused of being behind the assassination were Lansky subordinates. Perhaps Oliver Stone failed to mention these details in *JFK* because his film

was financed by Arnon Milchan, an Israeli arms dealer linked to smuggling of materiel to Israel's nuclear program—the point of contention between JFK and Israel. Although Israeli diplomat Uri Palti called Piper's thesis "nonsense," and pro-Israel columnist George Will declared it "vicious intellectual licentiousness," *The Los Angeles Times* grudgingly admitted that *Final Judgment* was "novel indeed," saying it "weave[s] together some of the key threads in a tapestry that many say is unique." The very week in 1997 the American Library Association sponsored "Banned Books Week," the Anti-Defamation League—a leading cog in the Israeli lobby—created an uproar, forcing cancellation of a college seminar on the JFK assassination because Piper had been invited to speak. The ADL feared "impressionable" students might take Piper seriously, but they believed those same kids were old enough to fight in foreign wars to protect Israel.

Index

An effort has been made to make this index as broad-ranging as possible. Although the index largely focuses on proper names, there has also been an effort to include some subject listings, along with cross-references. Unfortunately, because of the fact that the "neo-conservative" movement in the United States has become so intermeshed with that of the hard-right Likud bloc in Israel, along with Jewish and Christian fundamentalist groups, both foreign and domestic, the distinctions often become quite blurred. Indeed, the truth is that the term "Israeli lobby" itself has almost become synonymous with that of the term "neo-conservative network." And although the neo-conservatives often howl hysterically that "neo-conservative" is often used as a subtle way of describing someone who is Jewish, nothing could be further from the truth, particularly since some of the most fervent critics of the neo-conservatives and of Israeli excesses happen to be Jewish. Despite all this, the index should prove helpful. We've provided additional explanatory material where appropriate, especially when it illuminates the character of the individual or organization being referenced. God—who is known, by the way, in the Arab world, as "Allah"— smiles on those who have the patience to assemble a comprehensive index. Persons whose photographs appear in the photo section are noted in *italics*.

Abraham, Spencer, 20
Abrams, Elliott, 13, 20, 27, 112
Allen, Andrew E., CIA and Mossad operative, 90
"American Empire" essentially a Zionist project, 99-103
American Enterprise Institute, 5, 12, 22
American Free Press (alternative national weekly paper), 14, 22, 32, 57-59, 79, 89, 92
American Jewish Committee, 38, endorses Jared Taylor: 88
Anderson, John, 80
Anti-Defamation League (ADL), 9, 68, 75, 79
Anti-Muslim and Anti-Arab hate-mongering, 83-90
"Anti-terrorism" propaganda and legislation (pre-9-11), 69, 80-87
Ashcroft, John, 68-69, terrified of calico cats and scantically-clad classical statues: 114
Ashcroft staff member attacks Gentiles as "goyim," 68
Bacevich, Andrew, 43-45

Bauer, Gary, 35, 116
Bennett, William, 20, 22, 35, 116
Big Oil & Zionism, 57-59
Bollyn, Christopher, 92, 115
Bolton, John, 9, 12, 13, 20, 55
Boody, Robert, 80
Boot, Max, 42
Bradley Foundation, Lynde & Harry, 22, 36, 37, 111
Bronfman, Edgar, 19, 51, 74, 110
Brownback, Sam, 72
Bryen, Stephen, 23, 29, 30-34
Bryen (Stephen) Espionage Scandal, 30-32
Buchanan, Pat, 35, 43
Bush, George H. W., 41-42, 58, and Mossad plot to kill him: 61; 119
Bush, George W., 2, 5, 20, 24, 40-42, 43-45, 45-47, as religious fanatic: 46, 67, allied with Sharon: 54-56, 57-59, 61, 66, 86, 91, 109, 119
Byrd, Robert, 11, 118
Clement, Richard, 27

Cannistraro, Vince, 84
Case, Clifford, 23
Castro, Fidel, 92-94
Center for Security Policy, 36, 38
Cheney, Dick, 12, 13, 34, 41, 86, 91, 113
China and Israel, 33-34
Christensen, Arne, 64
Christian Coalition, 39, 73
Christian critics of Zionism, Neo-Conservatism, 78-80
Christian fundamentalists allied with Jewish fundamentalists, 68-76
"Christian Right" & Neo-Conservatives, 67-76
CIA (and American racists), 88
CIA conflict with neo-conservative "Team B", 24-27
CIA funded American Trotskyites, 18
Clinton, William, 54, 62-63
Cohen, Eliot, 35
Committee for a Free World, 28
Committee on the Present Danger, 27, 28, 92
Council on Foreign Relations, 22, 35, 38, 39, 63, 64, 66
"Creative Destruction" of the Arab world (neo-conservative theory), 60-61,
Crowley, Dale, Jr., 78-79
Cuba (to be blamed for "terrorism"), 92-94
Decter, Midge, 29, 35
Delay, Tom, 72
Donnelly, Thomas, 36, 41
D'Souza, Dinesh, 42
Eisenhower, Dwight D., 93-94
Emerson, Stephen, 37, 83-84, 88, 117
Empower America, 22, 35, 38, 64
Falwell, Jerry, 59, 70-71, 78, 79, 116
Feith, Douglas, 12, 13, 34, 42, 49, 55, 71-72
"Fifty Unanswered Questions About 9-11," (report from *American Free Press*), 92
Final Judgment, by Michael Collins Piper, 122
Findley, Paul, 61, 119
Foxman, Abe, 68, 75
Fradkin, Hillel, 36
Franks, Tommy, 49
Friedman, George, said Israel was "big winner" on 9-11, 59

Gaffney, Frank, 36, 38, 72, 112
Gerecht, Reuel,, 37
Gingrich, Marianne, 64
Gingrich, Newt, 64, 117
"Goyim" (racist term used by Ashcroft-Bush staffer to describe non-Jews), 68
"Greater Israel," 2, 57-59, 67
Hannah, John, 13
Heritage Foundation, 81
Himmelfarb, Gertrude, 15, 29
Hubbard, Al 20
Indyk, Martin, 62-63
Inhofe, James, 72-73, 118
Israeli propaganda and "terrorism," 80-84
Jackson, Henry M., 5, 12, 23, 24, 25, 36, 78
Jewish fundamentalists aligned with Christian fundamentalists, 68-76
Jewish Institute for National Security Affairs (JINSA), 13, 31, 33-34, 42, 81, targets United Nations: 99-103
JINSA: see Jewish Institute for National Security Affairs.
Joffe, Alexander, 99-103
Johnson, Paul, 42
Joyce, Michael, 37
Kagan, Donald, 37
Kagan, Frederick, 37
Kagan, Robert, 6-7, 37, 53,
Kampelman, Max, 28
Kass, Leon 20
Kemp, Jack, 22
Kennedy, John F., 93-94, assassination: 122
Keyes, Alan, 116
Kissinger, Henry, 22, 38, 66, plan for world war: 95-97, 115
Krauthammer, Charles, obsessive-compulsive advocate for Israel, 8, 37, 42-43, 64, 117
Kristol, Irving, 15, 17, 18, 19, 20, 22, 28, 35-39, 45, 81, 111
Kristol, William, 4, 5, 6, 14, 15, 19, 20, 21, 22, 29, 34, 35-39, 41-42, 45, 52, 63, 81, 91, 111
Kucinich, Dennis, 10-11, 118
La Haye, Tim, 59, 74-76, 79, 116
Lake, W. Anthony, 63
Laquer, Walter, 82

Ledeen, Michael, 29, 60-61, 82
Lefkowitz, Jay, 20
Lehman, John, 36, 37-38, 112
Lemnitzer, Lyman, 92-94, 115
Lewis, Bernard, 85-88, 117
Libby, I. Lewis, 12, 20, 113
Lieberman, Joseph, 52, 77-78, 118
Likud Party of Israel (allied with neo-conservatives), 2, 5, 12, 19, 49, 51-52, 54-56, 57
Lisker, Joel, 30
Luttwak, Edward, 82
Marcos, Ferdinand, targeted by neo-conservatives, 38
McCain, John, 20, 38, 62, 64-66, 118
McConnell, John, 20
McCloskey, Paul (Pete), 61, 119
Media attacks Vatican, 76-77
Media promotes "dispensationalism," 74-76
Middle East Media Research Institute (MEMRI), 13, attacks Michael Collins Piper: 121
Military targeted by neo-conservatives, 47-51
Moon, Sun Myung, 76, 78, 110
Moran, Jim, 1, 118
Mossad and JFK assassination, 122
Mossad plot to kill GHW Bush, 61
Mossad targets Michael Collins Piper: 121-122
Murdoch, Rupert, 5, 6, 19, 38, 64, 110
Neo-conservatives & "anti-Europeanism," 52-54,
Neo-conservatives & "Christian Right," 67-73
Neo-conservatives & new imperialism, 40-45
New World Order scenario by Henry Kissinger: 95-97
Nitze, Paul, 25, 27, 28, 35, 115
"Operation Northwoods," 93 (generally, 92-94)
Oppenheimer family, 19
Ostrovsky, Victor, 61, 84, 119
Overthrow.com, 89-90
Paisley, John, 26-27, 113
Pearl Harbor (9-11 as "new" Pearl Harbor), 91-92
Peretz, Martin, 38, 110
Perle, Richard, 4, 5, 6, 12, 14, 23, 24, 29, 30,
31, 32-34, 36-38, 42, 48, 52, 55, 78, 92, 112
Pike, Winston "Ted" and Alynn, 79
Piper, Michael Collins, targeted by Mossad: 121-122
Pipes, Daniel, 25, 115
Pipes, Richard, 25
Podhoretz, Norman, 29, 35, 38, 45-47, 88, 111
Podhoretz, John, 35, 38, 111
Pomerantz, Steve, 84
Powell, Colin, 12, 21, 49, 120
Preston, Don, 80
"Preterist" movement, 79-80
Project for the New American Century, 6, 22, 36, 37, 41, 91
Quayle, Dan 6, 20
Reagan, Ronald (and neo-conservatives), 5, 12, 16, 18, 19, 28-29, 31, 32-33, 38, 46
Rees, Matthew, 20
Revell, Oliver (Buck), 84
Rittenhouse, E. Stanley, 79
Robertson, Pat, 59, 79, 116
Rockefeller family, 22, 63
Rockefeller, Nelson, 33
Rodman, Peter 12
"Rogue States Rollback" plan by neo-conservatives, 62-66,
Rostow, Eugene, 27, 28
Rothschild, Lord Jacob (and family), 19, 22, 63, 64, 79, 110
Royal Institute of International Affairs, 22, 63
Rumsfeld, Donald, 29, 49, 50, 86, 87, 91, 113
Saba, Michael, 30, 32, 114
Safire, William, 64
Scaife, Richard Mellon, 84
Schiller, Rabbi Meyer, 90
Schumer, Charles, 68-69
Scofield, Cyrus, 79
Scully, Matthew, 20
September 11, 2001 terrorist attacks, 59, 91-92, 94
Shahak, Israel, 59
Sharon, Ariel, 2, 5, 8, 9, 36, 51, allied with Bush: 54-57, 67, 109
Shattan, Joseph, 20
Solarz, Stephen, 38

Steyn, Mark, 42

St. George, Andrew, 24, 26, 32, 114

"Team B" Affair, 24-27, 92

"Terrorism Industry" (pre-9-11), 80-83

Trotsky, Leon (and Trotskyites), 15-17, 18, 33

Troy, Tevi, (Ashcroft staffer-turned-Bush advisor called non-Jews "goyim"), 68

US racists attack Arabs, Muslims, 88-90

U.S.S. Liberty, 39

USSR (Neo-conservatives misrepresent Soviet intentions), 24-27, 29

Taylor, Jared, 88-90, endorsed by Rabbi Meyer Schiller, 90

United Nations targeted by neo-cons, 99-103

Vatican targeted by neo-conservatives, media, 76-77

Vidal, Gore, 17

Walker, Charls, 28

Walters, John, 20

Weber, Mark, associated with anti-Arab agitator: 90

Weber, Vin, 22, 38, 64, 117

Wehner, Peter, 20

White, Bill (overthrow.com) 89-90

Wittmann, Marshall, 39

Wohlstetter, Albert, 24

Wolfowitz, Paul, 12, 13-14, 20, 21, 22, 23, 25, 34, 35, 36, 38, 41, 42, 49, 50, moves against military: 50-51, 71, 72, 86, 87, 91, 113

Wurmser, David, 12, 55,

Wurmser, Meyrav, 12

World Jewish Congress, 51, 74

Zakheim, Dov, 12

Zionism & the new imperialism, 45-47, 51-52, 54-56, 57-59,

Zionism & Big Oil, 57-59

Zuckerman, Mortimer, 110, 120

Order extra copies of **The High Priests of War** *to alert friends, family and civic groups to the dangers posed by the neo-conservative power network that dragged America into the disastrous debacle in Iraq.*

In *The High Priests of War*, author Michael Collins Piper has come forth with what is indisputably the first full-length exposition of the little-known history of the neo-conservative warmongers inside the Bush administration who orchestrated the war against Iraq.

Order extra copies of *The High Priests of War* (softcover, 144 pages, item #2000) using the coupon below. One copy is $19.95; two copies are $35; three copies are $45; five copies are $60. For six copies or more, please call Anne at 202-547-5585 for bulk/carton rates. Send payment to AFP, 645 Pennsylvania Avenue SE, Suite 100, Washington, D.C. 20003 or call AFP at 1-888-699-NEWS (6397) toll free to charge to Visa or MasterCard.

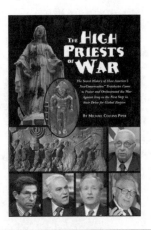

A LETTER FROM THE AUTHOR:

MICHAEL COLLINS PIPER
P.O. BOX 15728
WASHINGTON, DC 20003
EMAIL: PIPERM@LYCOS.COM

Dear Reader:

My first book, FINAL JUDGMENT, essentially explained how and why the Israeli lobby managed to become so powerful in Washington—a direct consequence of the JFK assassination.

There are, of course, those who refuse (for reasons I understand) to acknowledge that my charge that Israel's Mossad was a key player in JFK's murder is based on a solid and well-documented foundation.

However, what is <u>beyond debate</u> is that there was an undeniable and immediate 180 degree turn-about in U.S. policy toward Israel and the Arab world upon JFK's murder and the power of the Israeli lobby became entrenched as it had never been before.

In THE HIGH PRIESTS OF WAR, I've examined the hard-line "neo-conservative" forces that constitute the backbone of the Israeli lobby today. They have exercised their power in a manner that has led to tragedy for America and the world and which is certain to lead to further disasters in the near future. <u>They are shameless criminals of the worst sort and I do not hesitate to say it.</u>

Writing about these subjects is "radical" and "controversial," but, as they say, it's a dirty job and someone has to do it. I make no apologies for telling the truth.

That's why I have appreciated the continuing expressions of support <u>and</u> constructive criticism I've received from my readers over the years. I always look forward to your e-mails and letters and hearing what you have to say.

Sincerely,

[signature]

MICHAEL COLLINS PIPER